$22.^{95}$

A Guide to Collecting
Christian and Judaic Religious Artifacts

by

Penny Forstner

and

Lael Bower

Cover Photo Artifacts Courtesy of
Glenn Cavadel
Adele Cavadel
and Authors

ISBN 0-89689-113-5

BOOKS AMERICANA
INC.

This Book is Dedicated to

Our Father

Joseph DePelsMaeker

who is fondly remembered

and

dearly missed

Table of Contents

Christian

Judaic

Acknowledgements

Some of the items in this book are from the collections of the authors and the following collectors:

Fred Kelly

Bernice Sala

Virginia L. Abdella

Jesus Salas

A very special Thank you to Maryanne Dolan for her help getting us started.

To just say thank you to SOTHEBY'S of TEL AVIV doesn't seem to be enough. They are absolutely wonderful to talk to and they went out of their way to provide us with pictures of Judaic items that we could use. We are very grateful to them for their help, kindness, availability, and for just plain caring about what we were doing with this book.

We would like to extend a warm thank you to Ellen Debore of Christie's of New York for the research she did for us. She was a very bright light on a very bad day, and we will always be thankful for her warmth and cheerful disposition.

We would also like to say thank you to Swann Galleries of New York for the beautiful pictures they provided us with. Even though they were swamped with work, they took the time from their schedule to help.

We also want to thank Paul Diviovanni from the Autom for allowing us to use the DOLIF COLLECTION, and other pictures, and for allowing us to reprint some of their articles. They have a very friendly staff at the Autom who were always willing to assist us.

We also wish to thank the following for their contributions:

The National Museum of American History, Smithsonian Institution, Washington, D.C.

Leaflet Missal Company, St. Paul, MN

Yale Sacred Heart Church, Yale, MI

Hamakor Judaica, Inc., Niles, IL

Golden Era Sales, Inc., Grayling, MI

The Norbertine Fathers, DePere, WI

St. Johns Catholic Church, Peck, MI

SyrocoWood Inc., Syracuse, NY

We also wish to thank the hundreds of dealers we have talked to, and also anyone that we may have forgotten to mention.

I also want to thank my husband, John and my daughter, Crystal for putting up with all the confusion for the last few months, and for supporting my efforts. Every time I wanted to give up, they kept me going. There are no words to adequately express how grateful I am for their help.

Note: Prices in this book were supplied by Sotheby's, Leaflet Missal Co., The Autom, Hamakor, Swann Galleries, and from the sale of the same or similar items in galleries, auctions and flea markets. These prices are meant only as a guide, and may vary from area to area.

Preface

My sister and I grew up in an age when religious articles weren't considered art or collectibles, they were necessities. A Crucifix hung on the front door to tell the world that this house was a Christian household.

When someone would come to visit, Holy water fonts greeted them inside the door. Beautiful pictures of Jesus and Mary hung on the walls and statues of the Saints graced places of honor in our home. These statues served a few different purposes. First, it was very difficult to do anything wrong with so many Saints watching your ever move. We had so many of them at home, that we thought that it was impossible for sin to get into our house. That is another of the purposes they served, they helped to protect us, and to foster a deeper devotion to God. They also served practical purposes. Everyone knew that if you wanted a baby, you appealed to St. Gerard. If you lost something, they you asked St. Anthony to help you find it, even if it was his statue that you had lost. If you needed to sell your house in a hurry, then you took the statue of St. Joseph hostage. You would take him out into the front yard, and bury him upside down and your house was as good as sold. Blessed Palms were placed behind the Crucifix that hung on every wall, and in the evening, Blessed candles were placed in the window for the safe return of love ones, providing the house was still standing when they go there.

Then, things began to change, and the beautiful statues and pictures we grew up with were put away. Now they are a curiosity to the children who wonder what all those things are at Grandma's house. It is this curiosity that is prompting the younger generation to seek out these religious items. The antique stores I've talked to here in Michigan have a hard time keeping religious items in stock. The religious stores that we have visited have confirmed that there is a tremendous resurgence of people desiring these items, and more and more people have started to collect then. Many of these items are being pulled out of storage and finding their way to flea markets and antique stores, where they are quickly snatched up. There are still plenty of good buys left out there though, and we wish you the best of luck in finding your perfect treasure.

Introduction to Christian Collecting

Collecting religious articles is not a new concept. Since the very early ages, people have kept sacred items in their possession, and passed them down through the generations.

In the beginning, collecting religious items was meant as a means of protecting these items from destruction. Even with the brave attempts made to preserve these items, much of the early art work has been lost. Some of it was destroyed in wars, some by the weather, some by pillage, and some by the Protestant reform. Still, some of it was hidden away and has been copied and recopied over the years.

Some of the earliest artwork in Christian history can be attributed to the Veil of Veronica. Jesus left an imprint of his face on her veil when she wiped his face during the crucifixion. Artists copied the image from the veil, and legend has it that this is the reason for the similarities in the images of Jesus pictures.

The early Christians suffered many trials and early artwork served practical purposes during this time. Many different symbols were used to tell the faithful where they could find a friend, or to mark the graves of the Martyrs in hopes of preventing desecration. This method was used for many years before Christians could come out into the open without fear of being killed for their beliefs. Their artwork was also used as a teaching tool. Books were very expensive, and very scarce, but the people could read a picture much the same way that we read books. One problem that has arisen from this practice is that during their time the person in the painting was very well known, so they did not bother to write down who it was. This led to some problems in identification of early artwork, and sometimes it took years before the subject was identified.

The image of Mary also has its roots deep in early Christian artwork. Legend has it that St. Luke was a painter, and he painted several pictures of the Blessed Virgin. His pictures were copied over and over for many generations and the image we know of Mary is said to have come from these paintings.

Jesus and Mary are the subject of many pictures with the Sacred Heart of Jesus being the most popular. This picture has been done and redone thousands of times. There are almost endless variations to the pictures, and it is still being painted today as modern artists add their own touches. The crucifixion is also a very popular picture. This painting has been done from the very mild to the very dramatic as artists have tried to portray their own rendition of the event.

As interest in collecting Christian items grows, more and more items are being reproduced. Most dealers will agree that anything that is over 100 years old is an antique and the antique label alone is enough to increase the value. It is very difficult to give antique status to items that are mass produced. Still, there are many items that are becoming scarce. Dealers have destroyed prints for years to resell the frames. People have thrown out statues thinking that they weren't worth anything, and many items are still being destroyed today. Manufacturing processes have also changed, and most collectors prefer the older items vs. the new, so the demand for these items grows.

Most collectors desire items from the turn of the century, or before. The trend in reproductions seems to be items of the 20 - 50s, and items from the Renaissance period. As you become more experienced in collecting, it is easier to distinguish between the older and newer items. Take time to go through the antique stores and flea markets and discover what they carry. This will help in learning about the differences. Also, knowing the person or dealer that you are buying from will help you to learn about the various pieces. We have discovered that the same picture, or statue may be in several different sizes, each one with its own value.

When you begin collecting, try to keep in mind that collecting is fun. Stay within your budget and only buy the pieces you really like. It makes no sense to buy a piece you can't stand to look at just because it may increase in value someday.

Christian art is ever old and ever new, always changing, yet always the same. It has haunted, thrilled and profoundly affected people for many centuries and hopefully, it will continue to do so for many centuries to come. Enjoy yourself, and welcome to the wonderful world of collecting Christian articles.

Chaplets

CP001: **Chaplet of the Holy Spirit.** Chaplet has red plastic beads. There are five groups of seven beads, with two large beads before and after each group. There are three small beads at the beginning. 14" L

Value: $10 - 15

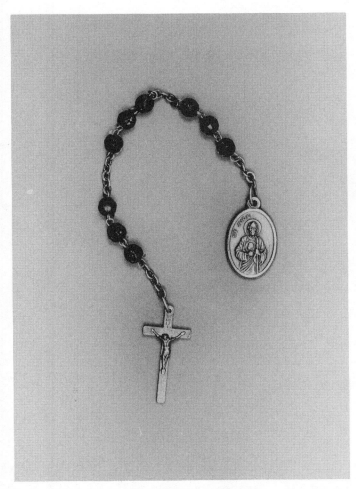

CP002: **St. Jude Chaplet**. Green plastic beads. Metal cross, gold colored chain. Three sets of three beads. 8-1/2" L

Value: $5 - 10

CP003: **Chaplet of the Holy Infant Jesus**. Silver capped ruby colored crystal beads. Silver chain. The medal is silver in the shape of the Infant of Prague. 8" L

Value: $25 - 30

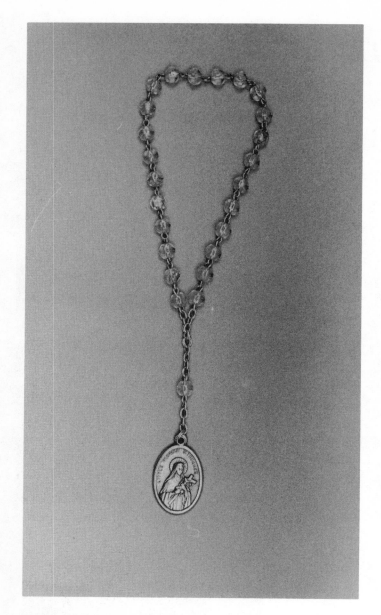

CP004: Chaplet of the Little Flower of the Child Jesus.
Pale rose colored beads. Silver medal of St. Theresa. 6" L

Value: $10 - 15

CP005: **Chaplet of St. Raphael.** Green colored beads. This Chaplet has three beads, then a circle of 9 beads. The first three are to honor Mary, and the remaining nine are for the nine choirs of Angels. 5-1/2" L

Value: $10 - 15

Crosses

CC002: **Sick Call Set.** Walnut cross, gold corpus. 13" x 8"
Value: $45 - 65

CC001: **Gold Crucifix.** This cross is 81 years old. Gold colored cross. Very Ornate base. The edges of the cross are also ornate. Metal 20" H

Value: $125 - 150
Photo courtesy of Bernice Sala.

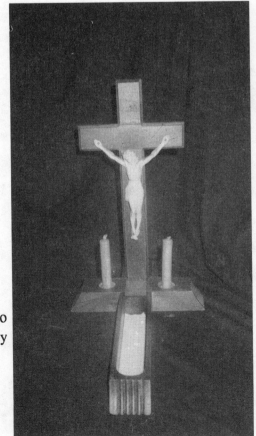

CC003: **Sick Call Set**. Maple cross, white corpus. Two beeswax candles are in the set, and a small bottle of Holy Water.
13" h x 7-1/2" w x 2-1/2" d.

Value: $35 - 45

CC004: **Sick Call Set**. Inlaid Mother of Pearl Cross. Jesus has brown hair, and a dark brown crown of thorns. He is wrapped in white. Gold ornate metal pieces are nailed on the ends of the cross. Cross is made from stained oak. Two 6" beeswax candles are in the set, and a small bottle of Holy Water. 16 x 10".

Value: $125 - 150

CC005: **Crucifix with Two-Tone Corpus**. This exquisite crucifix is made of beautiful walnut wood and features pewter-plated Corpus with arms outstretched and a golden halo above his head. 6 x 12"

Value: $40

Photo courtesy of the AUTOM.

CC006: **Very unusual Cross**. This cross was made from a fence post. It hangs over the door in the Sacred Heart Church in Yale, Michigan. The cross itself is a light brown color. The corpus is several different colors depending on the wood. 5' high.

Value: $5000

CC007: **This is a reproduction of an 11th Century Cross.** This cross was obtained in 1927. Cross is a light blonde color. Ornate designs down the center, and across the arms. 16" high.

Value: $65 - 75

CC008: **Sanctuary Cross.** Gold colored cross. 36" high. High polished.

Value: $920

Photo courtesy of the AUTOM

CC009: **Metal Cross.** The cross and Corpus are both silver colored. 7" high.

Value: $20 - 25

Art/Prints

CCP001: Madonna and Child.
Black and white lithograph.
8 x 10"
Value: $30 - 55

CCP002: **Jesus as a Child.**
Black and white lithograph.
8 x 10"
Value: $30 - 55

CCP003: **Jesus as a Child.**
Black and white lithograph.
8 x 10"
Value: $30 - 55

CCP004: The Holy Family. Beautiful black and white
picture. 16-1/2 x 22-1/2"
Value: $75 - 100

CCP005: Jesus with St. Joseph. Black
and white picture. 9-1/2 x 11-1/2"
Value: $50 - 75

CCP006: **The Holy Family**. Beautiful color lithograph. Jesus is in a white garment, tied with blue girdle. Mary is dressed in blue robes, and St. Joeseph is dressed in a red and gold garment, with blue shirts. "LITHO IN U.S.A." printed on the bottom.
14-1/2 x 9-1/2"
Value: $50 - 65

CCP007: **Jesus as a Child**. Very pretty picture. Jesus is dressed in a light blue garment. He has blonde, curly hair, and beautiful blue eyes. A small gold halo circles his head. 4-1/2 x 4"
Value: $25 - 35

CCP008: **Jesus as a Child.**
Black and white print. 7 x 8"

Value: $50 - 75

CCP009: **Infant of Prague**. A stunning picture that seems almost three dimensional. Jesus is dressed in a red robe, with a white collar and cuffs. The outfit is trimed in gold. He is standing on a silver colored stand. 19 x 15"

Value: $100 - 125

CCP010: **The Infant of Prague**. The colors in this picture are wonderful. The background is a deep blue, with gold stars. Jesus is dressed in a red robe, trimmed in gold. "Made in U.S.A., Copyright" on the bottom of the picture.

Value: $60 - 80

CCP011: **Christ at the Alter**. Christ is dressed in white garment, and the alter cloth is a beige color.
13 x 4-1/2"

Value: $75 - 100

CCP012: Very pretty color lithograph of **Christ with the Children.** Christ is dressed in a red robe, with a white coat.
11-1/2 x 9-1/2"

Value: $50 - 75

CCP013: Black and white picture of **Christ with the Children**.
10 x 8-1/2"

Value: $50 - 75

CCP014: The **Good Shepherd**.
Black and white lithograph.
10-1/2 x 8-1/2"

Value: $45 - 60

CCP015: **The Last Supper**. This picture is 60 years old. 18-1/2 x 80-1/2" L
Value: $150 - 180
Photo courtesy of Bernice Sala

CCP016: **Jesus in the Garden of Olives**. This is an oil painting painted by an artists who was in prison at the time. The picture was painted in 1948. The picture is signed, "G.E. Van Steenburo 48".
40 x 30"

Value: $325 - 400

Photo courtesy of Fred Kelly

CCP017: **Jesus in the Garden of Olives**.
Black and white lithograph. 10 x 8-1/2"

Value: $50 - 75

CCP018: **Jesus in the Garden of Olives**. This is a 3-D picture. Jesus is dressed in a white robe, with a purple coat. He has blonde hair. The colors are brilliant, and the picture is absolutely beautiful. 15-1/2 x 11"

Value: $50 - 75

CCP019: A color lithograph of **Christ in the Garden of Olives**. Christ has a white garment, and a purple coat. "Litho in U.S.A. No. 54", printed on the bottom. 10 x 8-1/2"

Value: $25 - 35

CCP020: Black and white lithograph of **Christ in the Garden of Olives.** 10 x 8"

Value: $25 - 35

CCP021: Oil painting of **Christ on the Cross**. "Dalblon 67" signed on the bottom.
22-1/2 x 16-1/2"

Value: $50 - 75

CCP022: **Head of Christ**. Christ is in a white gown. He has brown hair and brown beard. The background is black. His halo is yellow. The eyes follow you when you move through the room. 15 x 20"

Value: $100 - 125

CCP024: Lithograph of **The Crucifixion**. Christ is in a white wrap. The background is a greenish-blue, and there is red lines across each corner. 8 x 10"

Value: $30 - 45

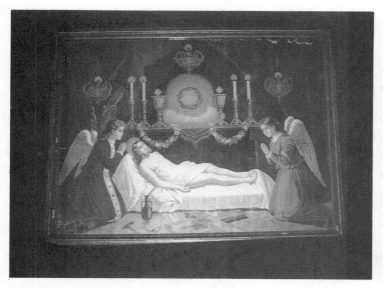

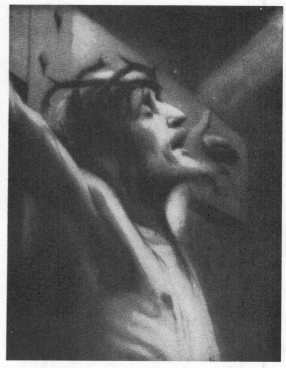

CCP025: **Christ lying on a white bed**. This picture was done around the turn of the century. Christ is lying on a white bed, with a white sheet draped across him. The Angel on the left is dressed in a very bright red gown with a white ribbon down the front. The Angel on the right is dressed in a deep blue gown with a yellow ribbon down the front. The oil lamps are red. 15-3/4 x 20-3/4"

Value: $150 - 200

CCP026: Black and white lithograph of **Christ on the Cross.** 8 x 10"

Value: $50 - 75

CCP027: Black and white lithograph of **Christ**. Picture has "*Holy, Holy, Holy*" printed in Latin across the top. 8 x 10"

Value: $50 - 75

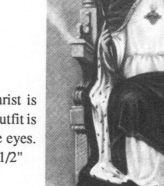

CCP028: A beautiful picture of **Christ**. Christ is dressed in a red coat, with a white gown. His outfit is trimmed in gold. He has brown hair, and blue eyes. The world is blue, trimmed in gold. 15 x 20-1/2"

Value: $175 - 200

CCP029: A black and white lithograph of **The Holy Trinity**. 8 x 10"

Value: $50 - 75

21

CCP030: Picture of the **Sacred Heart of Christ**. Christ is dressed in a white robe, with a red coat. He has brown hair, and greenish-blue eyes. 8 x 10"

Value: $35 - 40

CCP031: This picture is of the **Sacred Heart of Christ**. The picture is signed, and "copyright Edward Gross Co. Inc., N.Y. U.S.A." is printed in the lower left hand corner. The picture has a velvety feel to the material it is painted on. Christ is dressed in a white robe, with a red coat. He has brown hair, and brown eyes. His heart lightly shines through his robe. This picture is being reproduced today.

Value: $100 - 125

CCP032: Black and white lithograph of **The Sacred Heart of Christ.**
8 x 10"

Value: $40 - 50

CCP033: Picture is of **The Sacred Heart of Christ**. Christ is wearing a white gown with a light red coat. He has blonde colored hair, and blue eyes. The background is in gold's and browns. 11 x 9-1/2"

Value: $25 - 35

CCP034: Picture of **The Sacred Heart of Christ**. Christ is wearing a burgundy coat, with a white robe. He has blondish-brown hair, and blue eyes. A black background. 8 x 10"

Value: $25 - 35

CCP035: Turn of the Century oil painting of **The Sacred Heart of Christ**. Christ is wearing a white robe, with a light red coat. His Heart is prominently displayed outside the white garment. He has very light brown hair, and brown eyes. 29 x 21"

Value: $150 - 200

CCP036: Color lithograph of **The Sacred Heart of Christ**. Christ is wearing a light blue gown with a bright red coat. He has reddish-brown hair, and bright blue eyes. His mouth is a bright red, and his heart is also bright red with a greenish crown of thorns encircling it. "Copyright A96 Litho USA" printed on the bottom. 7 x 5"
Value: $35 - 45

CCP037: **The Sacred Heart of Christ**. This picture is 69 years old. Christ is in a white robe, with a red coat. He has brown hair, with brown eyes. A light brown background, and a gold circle of light over his head. The Sacred Heart Prayer is printed on the back. 8 x 10"
Value: $75 - 85
Photo courtesy of Bernice Sala.

CCP038: A pair of pictures of **The Sacred Heart of Christ**, and **The Immaculate Heart of Mary**. Pictures were done in the 1920-30's. Jesus is wearing a dark red robe, with a white coat. He has reddish-brown hair, and brown eyes. Mary is wearing a dark red robe, with a blue coat, trimmed in gold. She has a white veil, with a hint of reddish-brown hair. 22-1/2 x 18-/12"

Value: $125 - 150 pair.

CCP039: A pair of pictures of **The Sacred Heart of Christ**, and **The Immaculate Heart of Mary**. These pictures were bought in Detroit in 1952, and when they were picked up, the shopkeeper had cut them to fit these frames, thus losing the artists name. They are painted on canvas. 13 x 16" cut size.

Value: $30 - 45

CCP040, CCP040a: A stunning set of pictures of **The Sacred Heart of Christ** and **The Immaculate Heart of Mary**. They have never been removed from their frames and are in perfect condition. The pictures are extremely lifelike, and they follow your movements as you walk in front of them.
29-1/4 x 24-1/4" w/Frames

Value: $1500 - 2000

CCP040: Jesus is dressed in a dark red robe, with a dark blue coat, trimmed in gold. He has dark brown hair, and blue eyes.

CCP040a: Mary is dressed in a dark red robe, with a dark blue coat. she has dark brown, curly hair and blue eyes. A white veil with gold trim covers her head, and a halo of light encircles her head. She is holding a white flower, and white flowers encircle her heart. Her heart is pierced with a sword, and a white flower protrudes from the top of it.

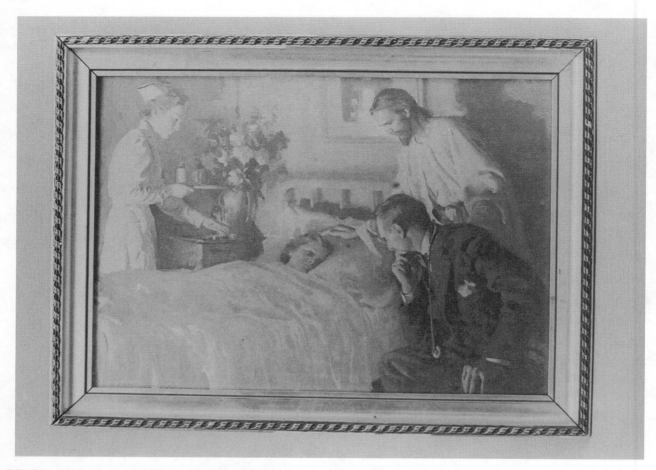

CCP041: This picture of **Christ at a Child's sick bed,** is done with greenish overtones. Christ is wearing a white robe, and has dark brown hair. This picture is being reproduced today. There is not as much green in the coloration of the reproductions. "Copyright 1952 by Medical Philanthropies, Lamalinda, Cal." is printed on the bottom. 15 x 20-1/2"

Value: $75 - 125

CCP042: Black and white lithograph of **Communion**.
8 x 10"

Value: $35 - 45

CCP043: Black and white lithograph of **Communion**
11 x 15"

Value: $50 - 75

CCP044: Black and white lithograph of **Jesus and Mary with the Children**.
15 x 20"

Value: $50 - 75

CCP045: Black and white lithograph of **Christ the Teacher.**
15 x 20"

Value: $50 - 75

CCP046: Black and white lithograph of **Mary and The Holy Spirit.** 8 x 10"

Value: $35 - 40

CCP047: Black and white lithograph of **Mary with the Christ Child.** 8 x 10"

Value: $45 -50

CCP049: **The Angelus.** Picture is painted on plasterboard. Gold and blue background. Girl is wearing a powdered blue skirt and brown jacket. The boy is wearing a pair of green pants and a brown jacket. 21 x 16-1/2"

Value: $75 - 100

CCP048: **Our Lady of Tears.** Black and white lithograph. 8 x 10"

Value: $45 - 50

CCP050: Black and white photo of the **Blessed Virgin of CZESTOCHOWA**.
16-3/4 x 12-3/4"

Value: $50 - 75

CCP051: Very pretty picture of the **Madonna and Child**. Mary has a light blue gown and a blue coat. Her veil is white, and a gold halo encircles her head. Jesus is unclothed, except for a white blanket wrapped around him. He has blonde curly hair. "Madonna of the Lilies No. 1036" printed on the bottom. 8 x 10"

Value: $50 - 65

CCP052: **Our Lady of Perpetual Help**. Mary has a red gown with a dark blue coat and veil. Jesus is wearing a blue gown with a light red coat. Gold background. "1748 L. SalomoneRoma No. 52 Made in Italy. ATTACA AD ICOMRN PRODIGIOSAN" is printed on the picture. 9 x 12"

Value: $25 - 35

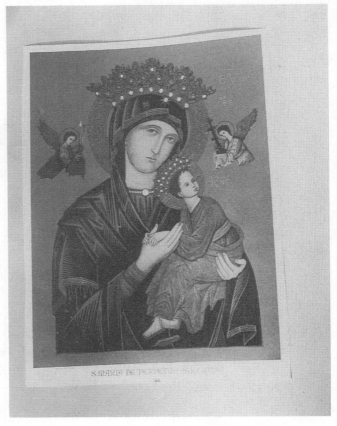

CCP053: **Mary with Roses**. Very pretty picture. Mary is dressed in a dark blue coat with white cuffs. She has a white veil, and light brown hair. The background is a light blue. 8-1/2 x 6-1/2"

Value: $20 - 25

CCP054: A color lithograph of **Mary in Prayer**. Mary is dressed in a dark blue coat with white insides. She has light brown hair, and green eyes. 10 x 8-1/2"

Value: $35 - 50

CCP055: **Our Lady of Grace**. Mary is wearing a white robe with a light blue mantle. Gold stars encircle her head. Her veil is white, her hair is a light brown and her eyes are blue. White rays are streaming from both her hands, and she is standing on a green serpent. 18-1/2 x 14-1/2"

Value: $95 - 120

CCP055: Black and white lithograph of **Mary**.
8-1/2 x 12-1/2"

Value: $45 - 50

CCP057: A beautiful black and white picture of **Mary's Coronation**.
22-3/4 x 20-1/2"

Value: $175 - 200

CCP059: **The Divine Mercy**. Jesus is wearing a white satin looking gown. There are rays of blue, red and white light coming from his chest. Dark background. "Jesus I trust in you" is written across the bottom. 9 x 11"

Value: $20 - 25

CCP058: Black and white lithograph of **Mary's Assumption**.
8-1/2 x 10"
Value: $45 - 50

CCP060: A black and white lithograph of **Our Lady of the Brown Scapular.**
20-1/2 x 16-1/2"

Value: $65 - 85

CCP061: Black and white lithograph of **Mary, Queen of the Martyrs and Saints**.
20-1/2 x 16-1/2"

Value: $100 - 125

CCP062: Black and white lithograph of **St. Michael**. 20 x 22-1/2"

Value: $125 - 150

CCP063: Color lithograph of **St. Michael**. St. Michael has a blue top, with a gold skirt. Light blue background. 8 x 10"

Value: $50 - 75

CCP064: Black and white picture of **St. Michael**. 16-1/2 x 20"

Value: $75 - 100

CCP065: Black and white picture of the **Guardian Angel**.
16 x 20"

Value: $100 - 125

CCP066: **Mother Cabrini, Patron of Immigrants.** Black and white picture. 8 x 10"

Value: $45 - 50

CCP067: Black and white print of
Our Lady of Fatima. 13-1/2 x 10"

Value: $25 - 35

CCP068: **Our Lady of Lourdes**. Black and white photo lithograph. 16 x 20"

Value: $75 - 100

CCP069: **St. Anne**. Black and white lithograph. "E.B.C. 142" on the picture. 5 x 7"

Value: $20 - 25

CCP070: Color picture of **The Guardian Angel**. The Angel is dressed in a white robe, with a blue sash. She has white and gold wings The child is dressed in a bright pink gown. Both have blondish-brown hair. Greenish background. 20-1/2 x 16-1/2"

Value: $125 - 150

CCP071: Color picture of **St. Therese**. She is wearing a golden brown mantle. She has a dark blue veil, and golden light shines around her head. Golden light streams upward from the cross. Blue-green background. 18 x 12-1/2"

Value: $75 - 100

CCP072: **St. Theresa**. Black and white lithograph.
8 x 10"

Value: $45 - 55

46

CCP073: Black and white picture of **St. Veronica.**
16-1/2 x 20-1/2"

Value: $150 - 200

CCP074: Black and white lithograph of **St. Thomas Aquinas.** 8 x 10"
Value: $20 - 25

CCP075: Black and white lithograph of **St. Vincent de Paul.** 8 x 10"
Value: $20 - 25

CCP076: Black and white lithograph of **St. Rita.** 8 x 10"
Value: $20 - 25

CCP077: Black and white lithograph of **St. Gerard Maiella.** 8 x 10"
Value: $20 -25

CCP078: Black and white lithograph of **St. Margaret Mary.** 8 x 10"
Value: $20 - 25

CCP079: **Paulus VI Pont. Max.** The Pope is wearing a red jacket with a white robe. He has a gold, ornate, stole. "21 June 1963-69 Aug. 1978" printed on the picture. Picture is painted on canvas. 8 x 10"
Value: $50 - 65

CCP080: **Pope Paul VIII.** Black and white picture. 15 x 20"
Value: $75 - 100

CCP081: Black and white picture.
16-1/2 x 20-1/2"

Value: $125 - 150

CCP082: Black and white picture.
20-1/2 x 22-1/2"

Value: $125 - 150

CCP083: **Pope St. Leo XIII**. The Pope is wearing a white robe and sitting on a red velvety looking wrap. Bluish-green background. 8 x 10"

Value: $35 - 45

CCP084: A beautiful picture from Germany. Written in German on the bottom is "For Thine is the Kingdom". Picture is dated 1910. 18 x 24"

Value: $200 - 250

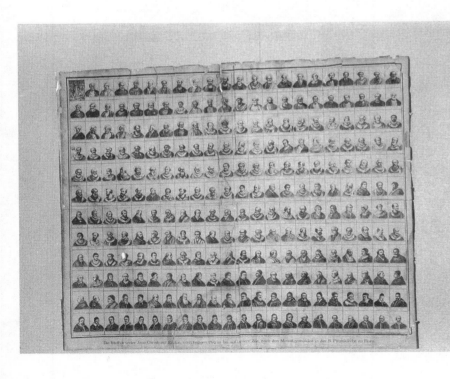

CCP085: **Peter the Roman to Leo XIII**. A black and white picture of all the Popes. "Ragensburg, N.Y. & Cincinnati. W. Schuffer Xyloga Austult, 1823-1829" is written on the bottom. 18 x 23"

Value: $450 - 500

CCP086: Black and white picture of **St. Theresa**.
8 x 10"

Value: $25 - 35

CCP087: A beautiful color picture of **a girl praying**. The girl is wearing a powered-blue outfit. She has brown hair, and a small gold halo encircles her head. She has blue, uplifted eyes. A reddish-brown background. 10-1/2 x 8-1/2"

Value: $65 - 75

CCP088: A stained glass picture of the **Madonna**. The picture has deep reds, and blues, with silver flecks throughout it. 12 x 9"

Value: $45 - 50

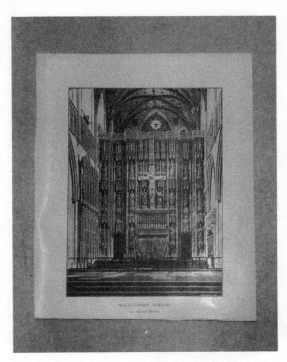

CCP089: Black and white lithograph of a **Cathedral**. Dated 1909. 8 x 10"

Value: $50 - 75

CCP090: Lithograph of The **Madonna and Child.** Reddish color. Dated 1909. 8 x 10"

Value: $45 - 55

CCP091: **Grace**. Dark background. The old gent is wearing a black shirt. His hair is gray. 17-1/2 x 22"

Value: $50 - 75

CCP092: **St. John the Evangelist.** He is wearing a Royal blue robe. He has dark colored skin, and blue-black hair. He is holding a red book. 20 x 28"
Value: $125 - 130

CCP093: **St. Joseph teaching Jesus.** Black and white. Copy of a print given to Pope John Paul II. 11 x 14"
Value: $35 - 50

Rosaries

RR001: **Mother of Pearl Rosary**. Silver chain. The center medal is Our Lady of Lourdes. Silver Corpus on the cross. 20" L

Value: $150 - 200

RR002: **Mysteries Rosary**. Made in Italy. Center medal opens to reveal the *mysteries*. Blue crystal beads with silver caps on the Lords Prayers. Pat pending on bottom of medal. 23" L

Value: $100 - 125

RR003: **Sterling Silver Rosary**. The entire rosary is sterling except the beads which are blue satin finished. All Lords prayers are double sterling silver capped, and all other beads are single sterling silver capped. Stamped Sterling. 21" L

Value: $135 - 150

RR004: **A Beautiful Sterling Silver Rosary**. The Cross and Medal are both stamped Sterling. The chain is Sterling, and the beads are cut Crystal. 22" L

Value: $225 - 300

RR005: **Mother of Pearl Rosary**. Stamped Made in Italy. Silver chain and cross. Our Lady of Fatima medal. 23" L

Value: $50 - 75

RR006: **Irish Rosary**. Square beads made from Connemara marble. Celtic cross had "Erin" stamped on the back. The medal has Mary on the front and Jesus on the back. Green color. 25" L

Value: $25 - 30

RR007: This **Rosary** is made of black seeds on a Silver chain. The seeds have a tobacco fragrance. Sacred Heart medal with Our Lady of Mt. Carmel on the reverse side. Rosewood cross. This rosary was given to a very special priest for his 50th Anniversary in the Priesthood. 24" L

Value: $100 - 125

RR008: **Christmas Rosary**. Silver cross, medal and chain. Red beads, with green beads for all the Lords Prayers. Holy Family medal with "pray for us" on the back. Italy. 19" L

Value $10 - 15

RR009: **Hand made Irish Rosary**. Green glass beads embossed with a Shamrock on each bead. Silver Celtic cross is stamped "Erin" on the back. Silver chain. 26" L

Value: $20 - 30

RR010: **Gold Crystal Rosary**. Crystal cut beads strung together with a gold chain. The cross and medal are also gold. The medal is of Mary. 24" L

Value: $50 - 75

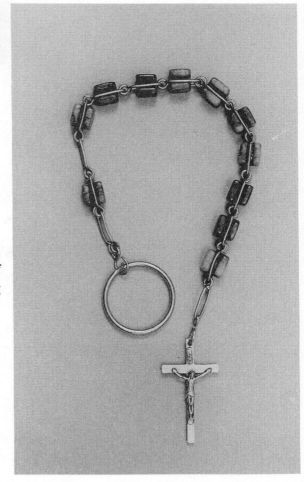

RR011: **Irish Rosary**. This is a single decade rosary used in the Penal days. The Rosary is made in Ireland of Connemara marble. Square cut green beads on a strong silver chain. Silver cross. 9" L

Value: $10 - 15

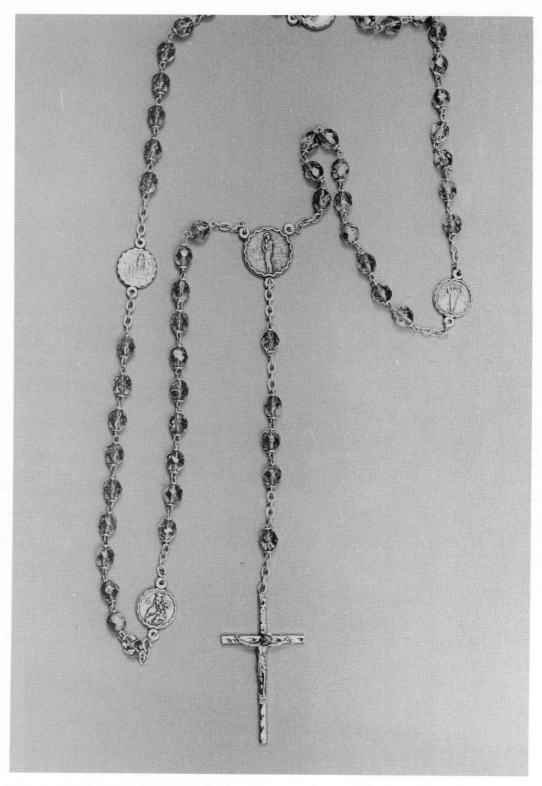

RR012: **Marian Year Rosary**. Blue crystal beads. Five medals from five different shrines of our Lady. Cross stamped Italy. The rosary is received for a donation. 23" L

Value: $10 - 20

Statues

RS001: Nativity Scene. DOLFI. 40"
Value: $1999
Photo courtesy of the AUTOM

Note: DOLFIS' skilled craftsmanship and total commitment to producing fine quality works of art have been a long standing tradition. In 1892 the DOLFI dynasty was founded by Franz Comploi, who carved and painted the first solid wood Tyrolean figurines. Forty years later, under the direction of DOLFI Comploi, the studio began to flourish. The Tyrolean tradition became known as the DOLFI collection. Willi Comploi followed in his father's footsteps and is the present owner of the DOLFI studios located in the picturesque Gardena Valley in Northern Italy. His marketing talents have led to many new innovative products in recent years. His lovely wife, Annamaria is the creative inspiration of DOLFI studios, and together they head the most prestigious carving studio in the world. The over 100 year old Tyrolean tradition known worldwide and treasured by collectors of fine statues continues today. Reprinted with permisson of Paul Diviovanni, the AUTOM.

RS002: **Risen Christ**. DOLFI.
48" relief.
Value: $999
Photo courtesy of The AUTOM

RS004: **Risen Christ**. DOLFI.
48" relief.
Value: $899
Photo courtesy of The AUTOM

RS003: **Sacred Heart**. DOLFI.
48" relief.
Value: $899
Photo courtesy of The AUTOM

RS005: **Sacred Heart**. DOLFI.
48" full round.
Value: $899
Photo courtesy of The AUTOM

RS007: **St. Joseph**. DOLFI.
48" full round.
Value: $899
Photo courtesy of The AUTOM

RS006: **Lady of Grace**. DOLFI.
48" relief.
Value: $899
Photo courtesy of The AUTOM

RS008: **St. Joseph the Worker**.
DOLFI. 48" full round.
Value: $899
Photo courtesy of The AUTOM

RS009: **Lady of Grace.** DOLFI.
48" full round.
Value: $899
Photo courtesy of The AUTOM

RS010: **St. Francis**. DOLFI.
48" full round.
Value: $899
Photo courtesy of The AUTOM

RS011: **Madonna & Child**. DOLFI.
48" full round.
Value: $899
Photo courtesy of The AUTOM

RS012: **Holy Family**. DOLFI.
48" relief.
Value: $1799
Photo courtesy of The AUTOM

RS013: **St. Anthony**. DOLFI.
48" full round.
Value: $899
Photo courtesy of The AUTOM

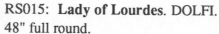
RS015: **Lady of Lourdes**. DOLFI.
48" full round.
Value: $999
Photo courtesy of The AUTOM

RS014: **St. Francis**. DOLFI.
48" full round.
Value: $999
Photo courtesy of The AUTOM

RS016: **Madonna & Child**. DOLFI.
48" full round.
Value: $999
Photo courtesy of The AUTOM

RS017: **Black Wise Man**.
DOLFI. 40"
Value: $895
Photo courtesy of The AUTOM

RS018: Standing Shepherd.
DOLFI. 40"
Value: $895
Photo courtesy of The AUTOM

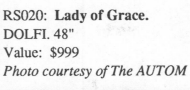

RS020: **Lady of Grace.**
DOLFI. 48"
Value: $999
Photo courtesy of The AUTOM

RS019: **Kneeling Wise Man.**
DOLFI. 40"
Value: $895
Photo courtesy of The AUTOM

RS021: **Wise Man Standing.**
DOLFI. 40"
Value: $895
Photo courtesy of The AUTOM

RS022: **The Holy Family.**
DOLFI. 48" relief
Value: $1999
Photo courtesy of The AUTOM

RS023: **St. Anthony.** DOLFI.
48" full round
Value: $999
Photo courtesy of The AUTOM

RS024: **The Madonna**. Hand carved wooden statue in a Mahogany color. 13"
Value: $200 - 225

RS025: **Pope John Paul II**. Wood carving in natural wood colors.
40" high x 5" wide
Value: $295 -350

RS026: **Moses**. Wood carved relief statue. Natural wood colors. 40" high x 5" wide
Value: $100 - 125

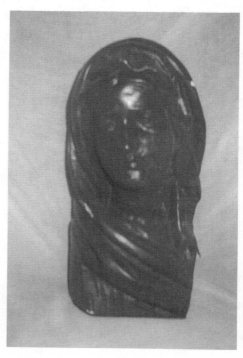

RS027: **Bust of the Madonna**. Wood carved statue in a cherry wood color. 8"
Value: $275 - 325

RS029: **Madonna and Child**. Dark brown plaque from SyrocoWood. This plaque is slightly bent. 1920-40's. 10-1/2 x 6-1/2"
Value: $100 - 125

RS028: **St. Theresa.** This is a beautiful plaque from SyrocoWood. The plaque is a dark brown in color, and very ornate. I called SyrocoWood about this plaque. They informed me that they quit using this method of making plaques many years ago. These plaques are becoming very difficult to come by, and it is extremely hard to find one in very good condition. Era: 1920-1940's. 18-1/2 x 8"
Value: $225 - 300

RS030: **St. Peter and Moses.** Identified by the Christian symbols of the keys of the kingdom, and the 10 commandments. Pressed wood look in a plaster cast. 20" high x 4" wide
Value: $ 50 - 75

RS031: **Nuestra Senora De Querna Vaca**.
Terra Cotta type clay art with the appearance of
hand carved wood. Red color. 18"
Value: $50 - 65

RS032:**St Joseph**. According to the annals of St. Joseph, this statue
is more than 100 years old. It was purchased in 1888. In 1889 a fire
destroyed the church, but not the statue. In 1892, two crowns were
made by a jeweler in Providence, RI and were blessed by the local
Bishop. The Premonstratensian Fathers of Saint Norbert Abbey
became custodians of this treasure in 1898. In the base of the statue
the following words are inscribed: "BAYERISCHE KONIGLLICHE
HOFKUNDANSTALT". Translated into English it means, "Bavar-
ian Royal Court Art Institute Munich". 5' 6" high and 5' 10"
including the base.
Value: Undetermined.
*Photo courtesy of The Norbertine Fathers, St. Norbert Abbey,
Wisconsin.*
If anyone has any information regarding this statue, would they
please contact the author of this book.

RS033: **St. Michael**. A beautiful pewter statue. The statue has been hand painted, and it was made in Italy. Set on a wooden base. 10"

Value: $47
Photo courtesy of the Leaflet Missal Company.

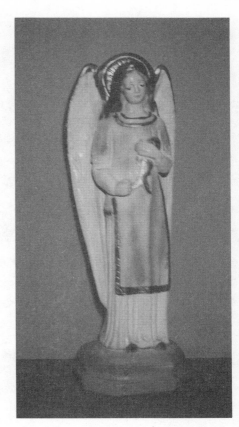

RS034: **St. Raphael**. This particular Angel has been venerated for years in both the Christian and Jewish traditions. He is wearing a white robe, with a lavender overlay. His wings are pink trimmed in gold. Gold halo, and he is holding a silver fish. 11"

Value: $50 - 75

RS035: **Guardian Angel**. Angel is wearing a white robe with a blue collar and sash. She has reddish blonde hair, and pink and white wings. Baby is nude. 7"

Value: $50 - 75

RS036: **Straw Angel**. Wooden head, no facial features. Carved wooden wings. 9"

Value: $35 - 45

71

RS037: **Madonna and Child with Angels.** Madonna has a pink gown with a blue mantle, blonde hair and a white halo. The Angels have blonde hair and blue wings. They have blue cuffs on pink gowns and blue collars. Madonna 10-1/2" Angels 4-1/2"

Value: $25 - 35

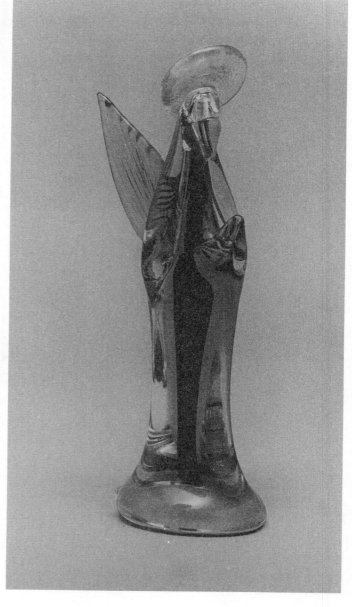

RS038: **A beautiful glass Angel.** The Angel is bluish in color. She had a bright red streak running up through her middle. Her wings are gold, and she has a gold halo. No facial features. 9"

Value: $175 - 200

RS039: A Musical statue of a Nun. Sister is wearing a powdered blue gown and habit. Her collar is white. She has a painted gold cross around her neck, and a painted gold rosary on her side. The base is white. Plays "AVA MARIA". 9-1/2" including base

Value: $45 - 60

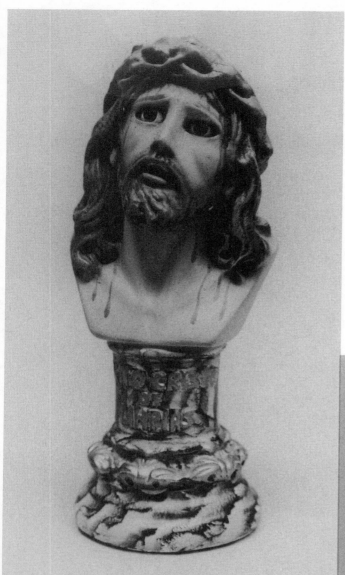

RS040: **Head of Christ.** This statue was bought in Portugal several years ago. Christ has a greenish brown crown of thorns and brown hair. He has brown crystal eyes. The base is silver and gold. 8"

Value: $150 - 225

RS041: **Head of Christ.** Christ has a greenish crown of thorns and brown hair. He has on a red collar and the base of the statue is white and gold.
7-1/2 x 5-1/2"

Value: $25 - 35

RS042: This porcelain bisque **night light** is cool and serene. A beauty to behold in the dark. White Madonna with a light blue veil holds a delicate pink rose of high luster in her hands. 7 x 4-1/2"

Value: $24
Photo courtes of The AUTOM

RS043: **Good Shepherd Music Box.** Christ is wearing a red gown with a white cloak. He has reddish brown hair. The base of the statue is green. Set on a wooden base. Plays the 23rd Psalm. 8 x 5"
Value: $75 - 90

RS044: A beautiful **Statue of Christ.** Christ has a tan colored gown with a red cloak. His hair is a reddish-brown, and he has outstanding ocean blue eyes. Blue base. "Roman Italy, 23896" 12-1/2"
Value: $325 - 350

RS045: **Head of Christ**. This statue was purchased in Portugal. Christ has brown hair, and crystal eyes. The base is gold and silver. 9"
Value: $125 - 150

RS046: **Infant of Prague**. Jesus is wearing a white gown trimmed in gold. He is dressed in a brown gown. A gold crown made from tin, with red rhinestones. 14"
Value: $50 - 75

RS047: **Infant of Prague**. This is a solid piece statue. Jesus is wearing a blue and red cloak, trimmed in gold. His gown is white. He has a gold cross, and a gold heart locket painted on his chest. His crown is red and gold. Gold base. "H.M.A." on back. Hand painted, plaster cast. 12"
Value: $45 - 55

RS048: Infant of Prague. This statue is wearing a white silk gown. A lacy gold cross is embroidered on the front of the gown. His cloak is red, and white lined. His entire outfit is trimmed in a lacy gold-flecked trim. His sleeves are also trimmed with gold lace. His crown is gold metal, with red rhinestones. A red rhinestone is also in the center of the cross on the top of the crown. His hair is blonde, and eyes are blue. The world he holds is blue and gold. He has a gold band around the two fingers he holds up. 6". 10" with crown

Value: $35 - 50

RS049: **Infant of Prague**. This is a plastic statue. He is dressed in a pink gown with a pink base. He has blonde hair, and bright blue eyes. His crown is silver, and the world he holds is silver, trimmed in gold. 15"

Value: $25 - 45

RS050: **Infant of Prague**. Christ is wearing a white gown trimmed in gold. There are also blue and red flowers painted on the gown. He has a non detachable gold crown. There is a bright red heart, and gold cross painted on his chest. His eyes are blue, and he has rosy red cheeks. "Japan" printed on bottom. 7-1/2"

Value: $35 - 45
Photo courtesy of Virginia L. Abdella

RS051: **Infant of Prague**. This statue is made from metal. He is wearing a cream colored gown with a red back on his cape. His crown is not detachable, and it is gold and red. Gold base. His hair and face are also cream colored, and there are no painted facial features. 7"

Value: $20 - 25

RS052: White resin statue based on Michelangelo's famous carved pieta. 6"
Value. $20
Photo courtesy of The AUTOM

RS053: A beautifully hand-crafted, hand painted sculpture of the **Holy Family**. Joseph leaning on his staff and **Mary** tending her infant, stands on a genuine dark wood base music box. Rich textures highlighted in gold, give the figure real warmth. A top quality musical movement from Switzerland plays Silent Night. 7-1/2" with base.

Value: $75
Photo courtesy of the AUTOM

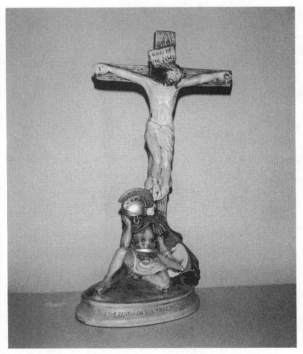

RS054: **The Centurion.** Hand painted ceramic statue. Jesus has brown hair, and the crown of thorns is a purplish white. The Centurion is dressed in a dark blue breast plate, with a red cloak. His helmet is silver, with blue plums. The base is brown. "And the Centurion said truly this man is the son of God" is printed on the base. 15"

Value: $65 - 75

RS055: **St. George.** He is wearing a blue breastplate and a brown skirt. His cloak is red, and his helmet is blue and red. Black leggings and brown boots. Holding a copper rod. 12"

Value: $20 - 25

RS056: Statue of Our Lady and Child. The entire statue is a tan color. A large "B" with an arrow through it is on the bottom, also, Germany is printed on the bottom. 9"

Value: $50 - 75

RS057: **Our Lady of Fatima**. Hand painted statue. Mary is in a white robe and mantle elaborately trimmed in gold. Her hair is black, and she has black eyes. The cloud is white, and the base is gold. 8-1/2"

Value: $25 - 35

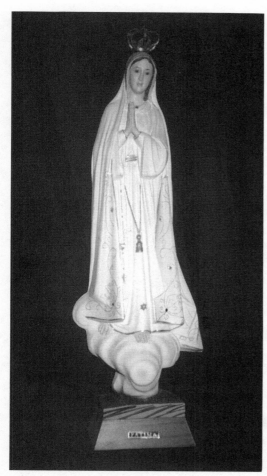

RS059: **Our Lady of Fatima.** Statue was made in Spain in the 1940's. She is wearing a white gown and white mantle trimmed in gold. Her hair is brown. A metal circle of stars is about her head. Her crown is gold over metal and detachable. The cloud she stands on is white, and three white doves are about her sandled feet. The base is marble. 12"
Value: $150 - 175
Photo courtesy of Bernice Sala.

RS058: **Our Lady of Fatima.** A very beautiful statue of Mary. She is wearing a white gown and mantle trimmed in gold. Her hair is brown, and she has brown crystal eyes. The cloud she stands on is done in pastels of pink and blues. Detachable metal crown with red, green and blue rhinestones. This statue is made right in Fatima, Portugal by Portuguese artisans. 21"
Value: $160
Photo by the Leaflet Missal Company

RS060: **Our Lady of Fatima.** This statue was purchased in Portugal. Made of Portuguese composition. She is wearing a white gown and white mantle, trimmed in gold and pastel blue hue to hem. She has a gold colored, jeweled, detachable metal crown. The cloud she stands on is pink and blue pastel colors. Three white doves sit on the cloud at her feet. 12"
Value: $125 - 150

RS061: **Our Lady of Grace**. Hand painted statue. Mary has on a pink skirt with a white top. Her mantle is dark blue, trimmed in gold. Her veil is white, and her hair is black. The earth she stands on is blue, with two white clouds. The Serpent is green, and the bottom of the base is gold. 24"
Value: $50 - 75

RS062: **Madonna**. This is an exclusive statue. There were only two made. Mary is wearing a gold robe. Her mantle is a beautiful dark blue. Her hair is reddish brown. She has a gold and white halo. The statue was made in Czechoslovakia over 70 years ago. 21"
Value: $2000 - 2500
Photo courtesy of Bernice Sala.

RS063: **Madonna Statuette**. Made of resin in rich brown/grey color. Her robes are flowing and fringed, her fingers and toes are perfectly detailed and there's a sweet look on the infant's face. 9-3/4"

Value: $20
Photo courtesy of The AUTOM

RS064: **Madonna**. Mary is wearing a gold robe, with a purplish blue mantle. Her hair is light brown. This statue was made in Australia. "Wien-Keranosi" is printed on the bottom. 23"

Value: $225 - 300
Photo courtesy of Virginia L. Abdella

RS065: **Nuestra Senora De Los Lagos**. A very pretty plastic statue. The Madonna is dressed in a light blue gown elaborately trimmed in gold. There is red flowers on the front. Her hair is black, and her crown is blue and gold. Two gold Angels hold a banner over her head. The base is gold. Made in Western Germany by W-Bein.

Value: $45 - 55
Photo courtesy of Jesus Salas

RS067: **Our Lady of Laleche.** This is a replica of the statue that is venerated at Our Lady of Laleche, St. Augustine, Florida. Mary has a reddish-brown gown with a white mantle. She has reddish-brown hair, and a white veil. Gold crown. "Mission of Nombre De Dios 1565" on the bottom, and "Our Lady of Laleche" is printed on the front. 5-1/2.

Value: $25 - 35

RS066: Bust of **Madonna and Child**. Mary has a blue mantle ornately trimmed in gold. There is a black and gold ornate front opening. Her hair is blonde, and her veil is blue with gold trim. The baby Jesus is in a white robe. He has light blonde hair. Gold trim base. "Made in Italy-034". 7.

Value: $75 - 100
Photo courtesy of Jesus Salas

RS068: **Immaculate Heart of Mary**. Mary has on a dark blue gown. Her mantle is light blue, trimmed in red. Her hair is light brown, and her veil is dark blue. The base is gray and silver. 12"
Value: $50 - 65

RS069: **Madonna and Child**. Mary has on a light pink gown. Her mantle is white. Her hair is light brown, and her veil is white. Jesus is wrapped in a light blue blanket. Brown base. 14-1/2"
Value: $50 - 75

RS70: **Madonna and Child**. Mary is wearing a white gown. She has a blue mantle and white halo. Brown base. 8-1/2"

Value: $50 - 75

RS071: **Our Lady of Grace**. Mary is wearing a white gown with a blue girdle. Her mantle is blue with pink undersides. Reddish hair, white veil. The earth is yellow and white, and the serpent is reddish brown. 10"

Value: $20 - 30

RS072: **Our Lady of Consolation**. Mary's gown is white, trimmed in gold. She is holding a gold rod. She has a blue mantle. Her hair is brown and her veil is white. Gold crown. Jesus is dressed in blue and white. Plastic statue. 9"

Value: $25 - 35

RS073: **Madonna**. Mary has a dark blue gown and a light blue mantle. Her hair is light blonde, her veil light blue. 10"

Value: $35 - 50

RS073A: Madonna. A very beautiful statue of Mary.

Value: $25 - 35

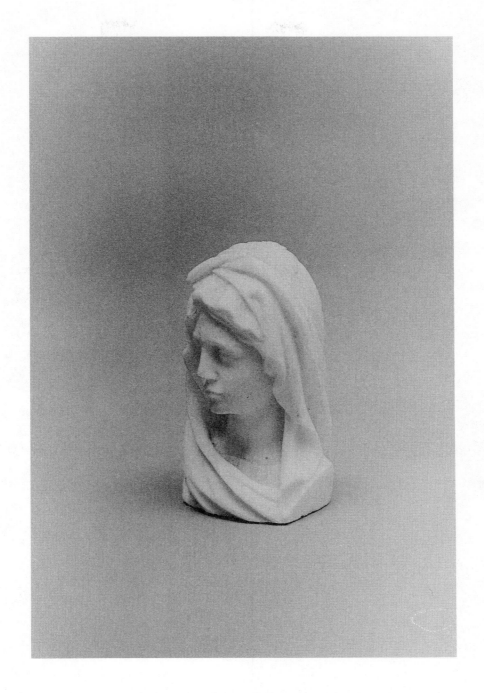

RS074: **Madonna.** White alabaster.
3-1/2"

Value: $25 - 30

RS075: **Madonna**. Mary has on a pink
gown. Her veil and mantle are light blue.
Light blonde hair. 8"
Value: $25 - 35

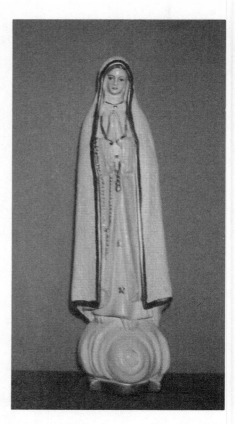

RS076: **Our Lady of Fatima**. Mary is in a light blue gown.
Her mantle is white trimmed in gold. The cloud she stands
on is bluish-pink. Gold base. 12-1/2"
Value: $75 - 100

RS077: **St. Theresa.** This statue was made between 1880 and
1910. She is wearing a dark brown gown. Her mantle is cream
colored., her veil is black. She is holding a brown cross with
a gold image of Christ on it. The cross is in the center of a
bunch of roses. She has a black and gold rosary at her side. The
base is gray, and two pink roses set on eash side of her. The
statue is painted plaster, and the frame is stained oak.
21-1/2 x 11-1/2 x 3-3/4"

Value: $800 - 1000
Photo courtesy of Virginia L. Abdella

RS078: Set of figures of the **Children of Fatima.** Hummel®.

Lucia is wearing a cream colored skirt with a light blue top. Her veil is white.

Jacienta is wearing a brown skirt with a cream colored apron and white shirt. She has reddish hair and a blue veil.

Francisco is wearing reddish-brown pants with a dark blue jacket. He has red hair.

H.K. 18-Francisco. H.K. 19-Lucia. H.K. 20-67-Jacienta.

Value: Not found at this printing.

Photo courtesy of Bernice Sala.

RS079: **St. Anne and the Madonna.** St. Anne is wearing an off white gown with a orange veil. Mary is in a light blue gown trimmed in gold. Her hair is reddish-brown. The book is white with gold trim. Gold and green base. 12"

Value: $25 - 35

RS080: **St. Anthony.** He is wearing a brown robe and has a brown rosary hanging on his side. His hair is blonde. The baby Jesus is in an off white wrap. He has blonde hair. Ceramic "A Napco Ceramic 5440-Japan" is printed on the bottom. 1930-1940. 12"

Value: $50 - 75

Photo courtesy of Bernice Sala

RS081: **St. Francis**. He is wearing a brown robe. His hair is light blonde, with a light brown band around it. Two white doves sit on his lap, one dove on his arm, and one dove on his shoulder. 6"

Value: $20 - 30

RS082: **Our Lady of Lourdes.** Mary is wearing a white gown and white mantle trimmed in gold. She has a blue girdle and stand. Her hair is black. St. Bernadette is all dressed in white. Plastic statues on a gold base. Filled with Lourdes water.   12 x 8"

Value: $50 - 75

RS083: Mother of Sorrows. Mary has a cream colored gown and blue mantle. Plaster. 24"
Value: $135
Photo courtesy of Leaflet Missal Company

RS084: Francisco & Jacinta Marto. Jacinta is wearing a brown skirt with a white shirt belted at the waist. Her veil is light green, and her hair is brown. Francisco is wearing olive colored pants and a brown jacket. His shirt is tan and his hair is brown. Their names are printed on the bases of the statues. Francisco 14-1/2". Jacinta 13-1/2"

Value: Francisco - $75 - 125
       Jacinta - $50 - 75
Not a matched set.

RS085: St. Rita of Cascia. She is wearing a black robe with a white collar trimmed in gold. Her veil is black, and she has a red wound from the crown of thorns on her forehead. She is holding a gold cross, and a gold rosary hangs from her waist. Gray stand. Plaster cast. 849 on back of the statue. 12"
Value: 450 - 75

RS086: **Flight into Egypt.** Hand painted ceramic statue. Mary is in light blue and white. Joseph is in a light brown gown with a dark brown coat. The donkey is gray and the base is yellow. 7 x 7-1/2"

Value: $40 - 65

RS087: **Pieta.** Mary is dressed in a white gown with a blue mantle. Her veil is white and her outfit is trimmed in gold. Jesus has black hair and has a white garment draped over him. Gold base. This piece was done between 1880 and 1910. 11 x 6"

Value: $75 - 100

RS088: Flight into Egypt. Mary has brown hair and a bluish-green veil. Her gown is pink. St. Joseph is wearing a camel colored gown and his coat is a light brown. "Made in Italy 820" on the bottom of the statue. 4 x 5"

Value: $55 - 85

RS089: Pieta. Mary is dressed in a blue gown with a blue mantle trimmed in gold. Her veil is white. Jesus has brown hair and is wrapped in a white garment. The base is gray. "Our sorrowful Mother" is written across the base. 13 x 7"

Value: $150 - 175

RS90: Jesus and Mary. A beautiful set of statues. Both pieces are a light tan color. They are both signed "A. Grammelli". 10"

Value: $100 - 125
Photo courtesy of Virginia L. Abdella

RS091: Madonna and Child. White pearl finish. Both mother and child have gold halos. "4-18 JO ANN" on the base. 11"

Value: $20 -25

101

RS092: **St. Philomena & St. Theresa**. St. Philomena has a pink top with a white skirt. Her cloak is green. She has brown hair and is holding a silver anchor. Tan base. St. Theresa is in a dark brown gown with a light brown cloak. Her collar is white, and her veil is black. She is holding red roses and a tan colored cross. Gray base. Each statue is 7"

Value: St. Philomna - $25 - 30
        St. Theresa - $20 - 25

RS093: **The Holy Family**. Hand painted night light. Background chapel is gray and light blue with a gold star at the peak. Mary is done in a very light pink gown with a white veil. Her hair is blonde, and eyes are brown. St. Joseph is in a powdered blue gown with a white cloak. His hair is very light brown, and his eyes are blue. The baby Jesus is in light blue. The base is gray and white. Ceramic. 18 x 9-1/2"

Value: $50 - 80

RS094: **Jesus & Mary**. Jesus has a light blue top. His hair is brown and eyes are blue. Mary has a dark blue top. Her veil is light blue. Her hair is light brown and her eyes are blue. Brown base.   7"

Value: $30 - 40 pair

RS095: **St. Maria Goretti**. She is wearing a brown robe with a white shawl.
Her hair is brown. Holding white flowers. Gold base.   9"

Value: $20 - 25

RS096: **St. Jude**. Plastic statue, tan color. 13"

Value: $20 - 25

RS097: **Nativity Scene.** White alabaster with two little Angels on each side of the outer edge. St. Joseph is in a very light pink gown. Mary is in a very light blue gown.
5-1/2 x 6"

Value: $50 - 75

RS098: **St. John the Evangelist and St. Anthony**. St. John is dressed in a black robe. His hair and beard are gray. He is holding a gold staff, and red Bible with a gold cross on it. A brown and gray bird is at his feet. St. Anthony is in a dark brown robe. He has a white belt and a gold rosary at his side. Reddish-blonde hair. The baby Jesus is in white. Each statue is 7"

Value: $20 - 25 each

RS099: **S.S. Giovanni XXIII**. White alabaster statue. 9" x 7"

Value: $50 - 75

RS100: **Jesus**. Jesus is wearing a dark blue robe with a red cloak. His hair is dark brown. Light blue background and a dark blue exterior. 7-1/2"

Value: $25 - 30

RS100: **Mary**. Mary has a red gown with a white belt. Her mantle is light blue, and her hair is light brown. Light blue background and a dark blue exterior. 7-1/2"

Value: $20 - 30

RS101: **Three Wise Men**. Ceramic candleholders. They are all painted a tan color. 6"

Value: $20 - 25 set of three.

RS102: **Three Nuns Candleholder.** All the nuns are dressed in black gowns with white veils. 4"

Value: $15 - 20 set

Miscellaneous

MI001: **Nuestra Senora De San Juan De Los Lagos**. White enamel with fluted ornate gold edges. The Virgin is wearing a white gown with a golden rose at the bottom. She has a blue mantle trimmed in gold with gold floral designs on the edges. Her hair is reddish-blonde. Her crown is blue and gold. Two Angels are holding a banner over her head with inscription "Mater Immaculate Ara Pronobis". Ceramic, made in Japan. A.R.A. on the back. 11" x 14"

Value: $50 - 75

Photo courtesy of Jesus Salas

MI002: **16th Century Last Supper**. Sacred Greek Icons from the ancient island of Patmos in Greece where artisans practice the ancient techniques of icon making. Generously laden with sterling silver and gold, then drenched in old world colors. Brushed with marvelous reds and deeps golds. 16th Century Byzantine copy. 19" x 13-1/4"

Value: $50

Photo courtesy of the AUTOM

MI003: **Metal plaque of St. Theresa**. Silver colored. Light pink on the roses. 6" high

Value: $25 - 30

MI004: **Metal plaques of Jesus and Mary.** Jesus is gold colored. 6" high

Value: $45 - 60 pair

MI004: Mary is silver colored and the roses are red. 6" high

Value: $45 - 60 pair

MI005: **Ornate Jewelled Chalice & Paten**. Faux rubies shine brilliantly from this gold-plated set trimmed in sterling silver. Features eight detailed scenes in the life of Christ. 9-1/2" high, holds 8 ozs. has a 5" diameter paten. Ciborium is jewelled with wheat and lily design. NOVA ARS BY THE AUTOM

Value: $2000

Photo courtesy of the AUTOM

MI006: **Plate of the Madonna and Child**. White enamel plate with a wide gold edge. Two smaller gold edges circle the picture. Mary has a green gown and a light blue mantle trimmed in gold. She has reddish colored hair. Jesus is in a red gown with a blue cape. Both have gold ornate Halos. This plate is between 65-70 years old. 9" high

Value: $100 - 150

Photo courtesy of Bernice Sala.

MI007: **Tassilo Chalice & Paten**. Hand carved by Italy's master artisans from sterling silver and gold plating, this exquisite set displays Matthew, Mark, Luke and John on its base. 7-1/2" high, holds 14 ozs. NOVA ARS BY THE AUTOM

Value: $4000

Photo courtesy of the AUTOM

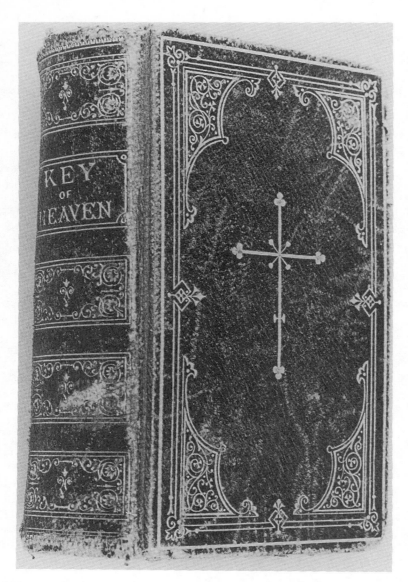

MI009: **Prayer book**. Black prayerbook with ornate gold trim. The Key of
Heaven or A Manual of Prayer. Approved by The Right Rev. Bishop
Fitzpatrick. Boston: Thomas B. Noonan & Co. Printed in 1873.
5-1/2" high x 3-1/2" wide

Value: $100 - 125

Introduction To Collecting
Jewish Artifacts

History proves that the Jewish tradition is one that is a survivor. The Jewish people have been driven from their homes, held in bondage, and persecuted for thousands of years. Even in our own time, they endured unspeakable horrors. Miraculously some of the beautiful Jewish artwork survived and began to surface.

At first, people thought that there wasn't very much of the older Jewish artwork left, and they bought all they could find. Since then, we know that there is a large amount of the older pieces that survived. Prices on the pieces were low. There wasn't much that dealers had to go by for setting their prices, so much of it was just plain guesswork. Then people began to take an interest in the Jewish pieces and pricing became more available.

The Jewish craftsmen learned that metal would stand the test of time. They realized that silver and gold were too soft to make things out of for everyday use, so they began to add copper mixed into the metals. Craftsmen began to add trademarks to their works, and an indication as to the gold or silver content. Knowing the silver or gold content allowed for setting a fair price on the piece.

One of the largest problems the collector of Jewish items faces today is that of forgery. Many pieces have been altered to increase their value. Some unscrupulous dealers may have added inscriptions or designs to plain pieces, or newer pieces may be passed off as much older ones. The best way to avoid this problem is to have any piece you may want to purchase checked out by a Judaic expert. If this is not possible, then it is always wise to know the dealer that you are buying from. This does not always indicate that the piece is not a forgery, but it does reduce the risk.

Some people who collect Jewish pieces use the pieces they collect. It is nice to be able to use a 16th century piece during one of the holidays if they desire to do so. Each collector has their own idea of what they intend to do with their collection. Some of them collect items that they know will increase in value so they can resell them at a later date, and some collect items to pass down through the family. It really makes no difference what people collect for as long as they reap the enjoyment. There is nothing like the thrill of obtaining a long sought after treasure, or of being able to show a beautiful collection to guests. No matter what your motives for collecting, have fun and good hunting!

Candleholders

CS001: Silver Sabbath and Festival Candlesticks
by Ilya Schor, 1959

Value: $77,000
Photo courtesy of Swann Galleries, Inc. New York

CS002: A pair of **Austrian Silver Sabbath Candlesticks**, Vienna, late 19th Century, each bulbous skirted stem set on a domed circular base, with pear-form candle socket, 38 cm high
Value: $1980
Photo courtesy of Sotheby's Tel Aviv

CS003: A pair of **Polish Silver Sabbath Candlesticks**, A. Riedel, Warsaw, 1886, each with a bulbous stem embossed and chased with grapevine decoration, with petal-form candleholders, set on a domed circular base with grapevine supports.
38 cm high
Value: $2420
Photo courtesy of Sotheby's Tel Aviv

CS004: A pair of **Silver Sabbath Candlesticks**, Russian, 1865, fully marked. 36.2 cm high

Value: $705,000
Photo courtesy of Sotheby's Tel Aviv

CS005: A pair of **Silver Sabbath Candlesticks,** Russian, L. Majerowicz, 1873. 29 cm high
Value: $1450
Photo courtesy of Sotheby's Tel Aviv

CS006: A pair of **Eastern European Silver Sabbath Candlesticks,** probably Polish, circa 1830-40, in Neo-Classical style, each in the form of a columnar standard set on a domed square base, the lower section applied with floral decoration, with removeable drip pans. 33.5 cm high
Value: $1320
Photo courtesy of Sotheby's Tel Aviv

CS007: A pair of **Silver Sabbath Candlesticks,** German, mid-19th/early 20th Century, struck with crossed swords above quality mark 13 and maker's monogram CB?, 20.5 cm high

Value: $14,950
Photo courtesy of Sotheby's Tel Aviv

CS008: A pair of **Polish Silver Plated Brass Sabbath Candlesticks**, Henneberg, Warsaw, circa 1900, each of typical bulbous form decorated with lions and Stars-of-David, the detachable drip pans similarly decorated, 32 cm high

Value: $800-1200
Photo courtesy of Sotheby's Tel Aviv

CS009: A pair of **Polish Silver Sabbath Candlesticks**, maker's mark MC, Warsaw, 1890's, each columnar stem with fluted knob and domed circular base with grapevine motifs, fitted above with petal-form candleholders, 37 cm high
Value: $1000-1500
Photo courtesy of Sotheby's Tel Aviv

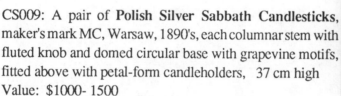

CS010: A pair of large **Polish Silver Candlesticks**, Warsaw, 1873, each with domed shaped square base, embossed and chased with flowers and scrolling foliage on a matted ground, the baluster stem and urn-form socket similarly chased, the wax guard with boldly beaded border, apparently no maker's mark, 39 cm high
Value: $3000-3500
Photo courtesy of Sotheby's Tel Aviv

Etrog

EG001: A **German Silver Etrog Container**, Johann Heinrich Ludemann, Dresden, mid-18th Century, of oval form, the body and hinged lid embossed and chased to simulate escallop shells, on three similar supports, with a moulded handle and shaped thumbpiece, later monogrammed,   10.1 cm high
Value: $5000
Photo courtesy of Sotheby's Tel Aviv

EG002: A **German Silver Etrog Container**, circa 1920, in the shape of the fruit, with a cast stem and textured surface, the hinged lid embossed with fruit and scriptural quotations in Hebrew for Sukkot, (tabernacles), on four orb supports,   16.5 cm high
Value: $1000
Photo courtesy of Sotheby's Tel Aviv

EG003: A **Polish Silver Fruit-Shaped Etrog Container**, maker's mark B.D., circa 1800, the lobed ovoid body engraved at one end with a flowerhead, the hinged lid with fruit and leaf finial, on four paw and foliate supports, also struck with a standard mark 12 and pseudo St. Petersburg town mark, 14.7 cm high
Value: $2500
Photo courtesy of Sotheby's Tel Aviv

EG004: An **Austrian Silver Etrog Box**, maker's mark P.S. Vienna, 1739 the oval body with end handles, fluted above the scroll supports with a matching cover centered by a later Hebrew inscription,   20 cm high
Value: $6000
Photo courtesy of Sotheby's Tel Aviv

EG005: A **German Silver Etrog Container**, maker's mark WH incuse, Berlin, circa 1830 of rectangular form with rounded corners, hinged lid applied with a band of stamped swans flanking shells, the top with further bird decoration, the front fitted with a lock flanked by two flower blossoms, all four spherical supports, some minor losses and repairs,   13.5 cm long
Value: $1320
Photo courtesy of Sotheby's Tel Aviv

EG006: An **Ottoman Gilt Brass Etrog Container**, mid-19th Century finely chased in the form of the fruit with foliage on a matted ground, the base decorated with an architectural vignette and applied with three budding stems, the hinged cover with fruit-form knop,
15 cm high
Value: $3080
Photo courtesy of Sotheby's Tel Aviv

EG007: A Fine **Silver Etrog Container**, Russian, marker's mark MS, 1861, traces of original gilding, marked,   14 cm high,   length of base 20.4 cm
Value: $5000-7000
Photo courtesy of Sotheby's Tel Aviv

EG009: A **Silver Etrog Container**, Austro-Hungarian, maker's mark I.P., Vienna, 1847, the interior gilt, 16 cm long
Value: $1870
Photo courtesy of Sotheby's Tel Aviv

EG008: A **Silver Etrog Container**, German, late 19th Century, marked on the base, 14 cm high
Value: $1760
Photo courtesy of Sotheby's Tel Aviv

EG011: A rare **Cloth Embroidered Etrog Container**, possibly Jerusalem, 1906, inscribed in Hebrew "The beautiful fruit of trees for the festival of Sukkot", standing on four porcelain feet, purpose-built glass and metal container, worn. This piece was executed as a wedding gift for Rabbi Shag Zwebner, 20 x 10 x 19 cm
Value: $1650
Photo courtesy of Sotheby's Tel Aviv

EG010: A **Silver Etrog Container**, Russian, maker's mark I. Sch., circa 1898-1908, marked on base and feet, 12 cm high
Value: $2875
Photo courtesy of Sotheby's Tel Aviv

EG012: A **Continental Coconut Etrog Container**, mid-19th Century, in the form of hedgehog, the body chashed with leaf decoration and animal face, the hinged lid with hook-form fastened with Hebrew inscription from Leviticus CH: 23 v-40, set on four silver claw-form supports,   14.5 cm high
Value: $1500 - 2000
Photo courtesy of Sotheby's Tel Aviv

EG013: **A Silver and Copper Inlaid Brass Cartridge Shell Etrog Container**, Circa 1920, cylindrical with domed hinged lid, the body applied with three blank cartouches interspersed with birds and scrolling foliage, set on three scroll supports, the base with stamped Hebrew mark "Bezalel Jerusalem",   19 cm high
Value: $1210
Photo courtesy of Sotheby's Tel Aviv

Hanukah Lamp

HL001: An Important **Continental Silver Gilt Hanukah Lamp**, probably Ukranian, mid-19th Century, the arched backplate formed as an ark, applied with four pillars flanking hands raised in Priestly Blessing below a crown, fronted by flower pots enclosing a row of eight lion-form receptacles, within a pierced gallery, raised on four tall scroll supports, the top with lions and gryphons flanking a crown, fitted with two latern-form servant lights, now contained in a associated cardboard box of approximately conforming design applied with a Menorah and dated 1880, *some old repairs, minor loss, struck with cross-swords town mark, datemark 1846 and quality mark 12*, 36 cm high

Value: $55,000
Photo courtesy of Sotheby's Tel Aviv

HL002: A **German Pewter Hanukah Lamp**, late 18th Century, the cartouche-form backplate pierced with a hole for suspension, fitted with a row of eight oil pans, the whole on four paw supports (servant light lacking),18 cm high
Value: $1760
Photo courtesy of Sotheby's Tel Aviv

HL003: A Fine **German Silver Hanukah Lamp**, maker's mark GSD and a heart, probably Frankfurt A/M, late 18 Century, the rectangular backplate embossed and chased in Neo-classical taste with foliate swags and borders, the top with open book entwined with swags and torches, fronted by a row of eight oil pans with hinged cover, the sides applied with foliate handles, all on four toupie feet, includes servant light, 18.1 cm high
Value: $12,000
Photo courtesy of Sotheby's Tel Aviv

HL004: A German **Silver Hanukah Lamp**, circa 1920, conceived as a tree trunk, the domed circular base chased with grasses and flowers, the naturalistic branches supporting eight fluted candleholders and matching detachable servant light, the center with bird-form knop, 25 cm high
Value: $2420
Photo courtesy of Sotheby's Tel Aviv

HL005: Oil-Burning Chanukkiah helps to evoke the ancient miracle. Kit includes eight glass oil cups, eight white tapers, bottle of kosher olive oil and box of 50 floating wicks. Solid brass Chanukkiah from Israel, 12" x 12"
Value: $85
Photo courtesy of Hamakor Judaica Inc.

HL006: A **Polish Brass Hanukah Lamp,** early 19th Century, the backplate pierced with flower filled urn, flanked by scrolls and surmounted by birds, lions and a crown, the side panels similar, with detachable vase sconces and a drip pan, applied with a row of eight oil fonts and pierced guard-rail, on four bracket supports, 22 cm high
Value: $1200
Photo courtesy of Sotheby's Tel Aviv

HL007: A **Polish Brass Hanukah Lamp,** early 19th Century the pierced backplate moulded with scrolls, surmounted by lions and birds flanking a crown, fitted with pierced side panels on four pad feet, each supporting a detachable vase servant light and drip pan, platform with eight detachable sconces and a pierced guard-rail, the back screw later, 23cm high
Value: $1200
Photo courtesy of Sotheby's Tel Aviv

HL008: An **Austro-Hungarian Hanukah Lamp**, maker's mark E.W., late 19th Century, the backplate embossed with two lions flanking a vacant shield for Decalogue below the crown and scrolling foliate border, fitted with a gallery and eight oil ewers, detachable servant light, on four cast supports, 21.1 cm high

Value: $1700
Photo courtesy of Sotheby's Tel Aviv

HL009: A **Bezalel Silver Hanukah Lamp**, circa 1920, the backplate in Hebrew these lights are holy below symbolic roundels within pomegranates and scrolls, flanked by pillars, crown cresting, the rectangular platform fitted with eight filigree girdled sconces and detachable servant light, embossed stamp Bezalel, Jerusalem on four supports, Also stamped sterling 925, 17 cm high
Value: $2100
Photo courtesy of Sotheby's Tel Aviv

HL010: A **Ukranian Silver and Filigree Hanukah Lamp**, maker's mark M.L.M., 1881, of "Baal Shem Tov" type the rectangular backplate with foliate scrolls surmounted by birds flanking a double-headed eagle (possibly later), with a servant light and vase sconce on a scroll bracket, fitted with eight oil ewers on a platform and four supports, 15cm high

Value: $3750
Photo courtesy of Sotheby's Tel Aviv

HL011: A Ukrainian Silver and Filigree Hanukah Lamp, Zhitomir, 1860, of 'Baal Shem Tov' type, the cartouche-shaped backplate incorporating pillars headed by rampant lions and flanking a crown, with two detachable servant lights and eight oil lamps attached to the base, raised on six supports, assay master Yakov Zlexeyevithch Davidov, 22.5 cm high
Value: $6500
Photo courtesy of Sotheby's Tel Aviv

HL012: A German Silver Traveling Hanukah Lamp, Berlin, circa 1830, the rectangular backplate chased with leaves, scrolls and flowerheads, centered by a basket, the oil compartment with a similarly decorated lid fitted with eight wick holders, leaf shaped grips and oval servant light, on four claw supports, 10 cm high
Value: $5500
Photo courtesy of Sotheby's Tel Aviv

HL013: A Moroccon Brass Hanukah Lamp, late 19th century, the arched backplate surrounded by a pierced gallery, stamped with crowns and chased with birds and Stars-of-David, the sides similarly decorated, with a detachable row of oil pans and matching servant light, 22 cm high
Value: $800-1200
Photo courtesy of Sotheby's Tel Aviv

HL014: A **Dutch Sheet Brass Hanukah Lamp**, first half of the 18th century, the cartouche-shaped backplate pierced, embossed and chased with hearts, roundels and flowers, centered by a servant light, fitted below with a row of oil pans above a rectangular catch tray, several old repairs, 31 cm high
Value: $2000-3000
Photo courtesy of Sotheby's Tel Aviv

HL015: A **Bohemian Cast Brass Hanukah Lamp**, Prague, circa 1800, the backplate pierced with rococo scrolls and flowers tipped trelliswork surrounding a circular cartouche decorated at the top and sides with three Stars-of-David enclosing Swedish caps, the sides cast and chased with Moses and Aaron, lacking servant light. The Swedish caps commemorate the Jews' valiant defence of Prague against the Swedish army in the 17th century, 19 cm high
Value: $1000-1200
Photo courtesy of Sotheby's Tel Aviv

HL016: An **Austro-Hungarian Hanukah Lamp**, maker's mark G. S., circa 1880, the triptych form backplate centred by a vacant panel for the Decaloque above a seated lion headed by a crown, the side panels surmounted by later bird's heads, embossed wiht lattace work and flowerheads, detachable vase servant light and a row of eight scones on a moulded platform, raised on four supports, 23cm high

Value: $2000
Photo courtesy of Sotheby's Tel Aviv

HL017: An **Italian Bronze Wall-mounted Hanukah Lamp**, 18th Century, the cast backplate of renaissance design, pierced with lions flanking a flower filled vase and scrolls, with a row of eight oil fonts, 16 cm high
Value: $700-900
Photo courtesy of Sotheby's Tel Aviv

HL0018: A **Bohemian Pewter Hanukah Lamp**, mid-18th Century, the cartouche form backplate pierced and engraved with wrigglework borders, the sides applied with two rampant lions holding a symbolic oil jog and servant light, fitted with a row of oil fonts on a scalloped shelf, the lower section with conforming engraved borders, raised on four spherical supports, some losses and minor damage, struck with two unidentified touchmarks, 20.1 cm high
Value: $4000
Photo courtesy of Sotheby's Tel Aviv

HL019: A **Cast Bronze Hanukah Lamp**, probably Moroccan, 18th Century, the backplate pierced with a row of mihrabs below stylized foliage and architectural motifs, with similar side panels surmounted by roosters flanking a row of eight oil fonts, servant light lacking, 22 cm high
Value: $1500-2000
Photo courtesy of Sotheby's Tel Aviv

HL021: A **Continental Silver Hanukah Lamp**, circa 1950, the shaped semi-circular backplate chased with foliate motifs, centering the Decalogue flanked by two lions, fronted by a row of eight crowned lion-form oil receptacles, each fitted with a funnel, the corners with crouched lions on plinths engraved with the Star-of-David, set on a rectangular base and foliate-scroll supports, the whole surmounted by a crown with detachable servant light and oil jog, both with lion-mask spouts, 29cm high

Value: $2640
Photo courtesy of Sotheby's Tel Aviv

HL020: **"Chassidim" Chanukkiah** by Ruth Block, quaint Judaic figures in there distinctive garb become elements of expressive art in the hands of sculptor Ruth Block. Chanukkiah candle-lighting time and year round. Oxidized bronze, brushed with gold, each piece signed by the artist, 10 1/2" x 7 1/2"
Value: $150
Photo courtesy of Hamakor Judaica Inc.

HL022: A **Bezalel Silver Hanukah Lamp**, 1930-40's, the backplate stamped in relief with lions flanking a Menorah above a Hebrew inscription fronted by a row of eight candleholders, includes light, stamped marks, 11.5 cm high

Value: $1870
Photo courtesy of Sotheby's Tel Aviv

HL023: A **Polish Brass Lamp,** 19th Century, the cast pierced backplate moulded with scrolls surmounted by lions flanking a crown, with fitted side panels, fronted by a row of eight candlesockets, all on four pad supports (one now lacking), includes servant light, minor repairs, 25 cm high
Value: $1100
Photo courtesy of Sotheby's Tel Aviv

HL024: An **Austro-Hungarian Silver Hanukah Lamp,** Vienna, circa 1880, the coartouche-form backplate embossed and chased with pillars flanking the Decalouge amidst floral swags on a matted ground below lions bearing cartouches, fronted by a removable row of eight oil jugs, the sides with scroll brackets, all on four panel and paws supports, 19.5 cm high
Value: $2000-3000
Photo courtesy of Sotheby's Tel Aviv

HL025: An **Austrian Silver Hanukah Lamp,** Vienna, circa 1850, the backplate pierced with flowers and rococco-style foliage, fronted by a row of eight spoon form oil pans above a drip pan, 18 cm high
Value: $2500-3500
Photo courtesy of Sotheby's Tel Aviv

HL026: A **Bezalel Silver Hanukah Lamp/Sabbath Candelabrum,** circa 1950, the double stem applied with filigree terminating into two candle sockets fitted with a row of eight candleholders/oil recepticles, includes servant light and funnel, the domed circular applied with filigree roundels alternating with 'eilat' stones, stamped marked, 31 cm high
Value: $1200-1500
Photo courtesy of Sotheby's Tel Aviv

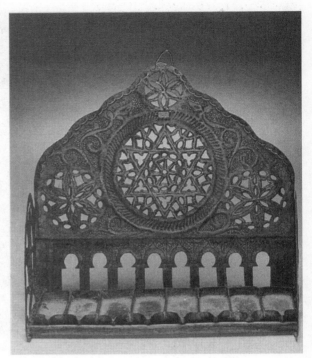

HL027: A **Dutch Sheet Brass Hanukah Lamp**, late 18th Century, the backplate pierced with a star within a boldly beaded border, surmounted by two pitchers flanking a leaf-form knop, the center with a lidded row of eight oil pans, repairs, 37 cm high
Value: $1760
Photo courtesy of Sotheby's Tel Aviv

HL028: A **Moroccan Brass Hanukah Lamp**, second half 19th Century, the arched backplate pierced with a large central rosette surrounded by scrolling foliage and three further rosettes above a row of mirhab arches, the sides pierced and chased to represent stalking wild cats, fitted with row of eight oil pans (servant light now lacking), 27.5 cm high
Value: $1200-1500
Photo courtesy of Sotheby's Tel Aviv

HL029: An **Istael Silver Hanukah Lamp**, Moshe Smilovici, Tel Aviv, 1960s, in Eastern European style, the backplate pierced and chased with lions flanking a Menorah, scrolls, birds and flowers, enclosing a central plaque with Hebrew inscription for Hanukah fronted by a row of eight oil cups/candleholders on a pedestal base pierced and chased with further scrolls and flowers, includes servant light, 24.8 cm high
Value: $1870
Photo courtesy of Sotheby's Tel Aviv

HL030: A **German Silver Hanukah Lamp**, maker's mark CLE, circa 1830, composed of a fabulous beast, the feathered-chased body terminating in eight heads, each supporting, set on two claw supports, the reverse applied with wings and terminating in scale chased fish tail, fitted with a servant light, 17 cm high

Value: $60,000
Photo courtesy of Sotheby's Tel Aviv

HL031: A **German Silver Hanukah Lamp,** early 20th Century, the tapering fluted stem set on conforming domed circular base, the upper section composed of two scrolling branches supporting a row of eight candleholders flanking a Star-of-David, includes servant light, 22 cm high
Value: $1800-2200
Photo courtesy of Sotheby's Tel Aviv

HL032: An **Austrian Silver Lamp,** maker's mark AW, Vienna, 1865, the backplate chased in the form of an eagle set on a perch befor a cartouche centering foliate scrolls and pierced quatrefoils, fronted by a detachable row of spoon-form oil pans, one side fitted with a servant light raised on scroll supports, some damage, 21cm high
Value: $3500 - 4500
Photo courtesy of Sotheby's Tel Aviv

HL033: An **East European Hanukah Lamp,** apparently unmarked, circa 1910, the swollen stem set on a domed circular base fitted with eight movable branches terminating in circular candle holders flanking a spherical knop and servant light, 41.5 cm high
Value: $1870
Photo courtesy of Sotheby's Tel Aviv

133

HL034: A **Large Silver Hanukah Lamp**, German, 1930's, the domed hexagonal base chased with fruit and flowers and set on lion supports, with four movable branches fitted with urn-form oil holders and matching servant light, centered by a Star-of-David knop, marked on base, 56 cm high
Value: $4950
Photo courtesy of Sotheby's Tel Aviv

HL035: **Silver Hanukah Lamp**, circa 1925, the section columnar stem with beaded borders, set on a domed square base brightcut with foliage, the upper section with eight moveable arms fitted with elongated urn-form candleholders, flanking a central eagle-form knop, (servant light now lacking), 63cm high
Value: $5060
Photo courtesy of Sotheby's Tel Aviv

HL036: A **German Silver Hanukah Lamp**, circa 1880, the rectangular backplate chased with scrolling foliate border enclosing a diamond pattern ground chased in the center with a floral fronted by a row of eight urn-form candleholders decorated with foliate swags engraved with a Hebrew inscription dated 1884, all on four panels supports (lacks servant light), 25 cm high
Value: $3740
Photo courtesy of Sotheby's Tel Aviv

HL037: A **German Silver Hanukah Lamp**, late 19th century, the domed circular engraved with Greek key bands and a monogram, the central stem fitted with eight leaf-applied branches terminating in candlesockets flanking an eagle-form knop (lacks servant light), 25.5 cm high
Value: $1100
Photo courtesy of Sotheby's Tel Aviv

HL038: An **Italian Brass Hanukah Lamp,** 18th Century, the arched, sheet-brass backplate applied with pillars supporting an arch, applied in the center with a Menorah fronted by a row of eight oil pans, the inside with matching servant light,
19.5 cm high
Value: $3300
Photo courtesy of Sotheby's Tel Aviv

HL039: A Rare Moroccon Silver Hanukah Lamp, late 19th Century, the rectangular backplate composed of pillars enclosing pierced and chased lions amidst foliage flanking tablets engraved with Hebrew inscriptions relating to Hanukah below a plaque with further Hebrew inscriptions, surmounted by birds and serpents, fronted by a row of eight oil pans, the sides pierced and chased with a bird amidst foliage, includes servant light, struck with Moroccon marks, 28.5 cm high.

Value: $9900
Photo courtesy of Sotheby's Tel Aviv

HL040: A **Dutch Sheet Brass Hanukah Lamp,** 18th
Century, the cartouch-shaped backplate pierced, embossed and chased with, roundels and flowers, fitted
below with a rectangular catch tray, lacks oil pans,
27.5 cm high
Value: $825
Photo coutesy of Sotheby's Tel Aviv

HL041: **Nickle Silver Tree of Life, Chanukkiah,** designed by Sandra Kravitz, who perfected her art in Israel
as a student of Yemenite silversmiths. 24K gold cups.
Velvet gift box.
6-1/2 x "
Value: $85
Photo courtesy of Hamakor Judaica Inc

HL042: The **Temple Chanukkiah** by Klara Sever, abstract art that can be interpreted as a group of heroic figures the Maccabees, sculptured by the artist with her characteristic dramatic flourish, hand-cast and hand-finished Durastone, heavy formica base, 15" x 15"

Value: $150
Photo courtesy of Hamakor Judaica Inc.

HL043: Alexsander Danel **"Jerusalem of Gold"**, Chanukkiah, handcrafted and hand-painted Durastone, 7" x 12 3/4" x 4 3/4"

Value: $125
Photo courtesy of Hamakor Judaica Inc.

HL044: Toby Maude **"Neighborhoods of Jerusalem"**, Chanukkiah, The Tower of David holds the shammash, includes houses from Mea She'arim, Mahane Yehuda, The Old City, The Jewish Quarter, Yemin Moshe, The German Colony and the Bukharian Quarter, 3 x 10-1/2"

Value: $140
Photo courtesy of Hamakor Judaica Inc.

HL045: **"Pillar of Life"** Chanukkiah by Fred Spinowitz, the noted New York designer reinterprets a traditional theme, from its strong twining roots to its graceful leaf shaped candleholders, this Menorah is modern gem, silver plate with 24K gold plate, engraved artist's signature, 10-1/2 x 12"

Value: $125
Photo courtesy of Hamakor Judaica Inc.

140

HL046: **Lucite Electric Chanukkiah,** using only one bulb, the individual "candles" are lit by simply adjusting slide controls on back of this modern Menorah, mirrors add to the dramatic play of light and shadows, there are two different models, one with multicolor light and one with clear lights, 11" x 13"

Value: $115
Photo courtesy of Hamakor Judaica Inc.

HL047: **American Bronze Hanukah Lamp** by Manfred Anson in honor of the centennial of the Statue of Liberty, 1986

Value: $8250
Photo courtesy of Swann Galleries, Inc.

HL048: **Bezalel Brass Hanukah Lamp,**
circa 1920

Value: $990
Photo courtesy of Swann Galleries, Inc.

HL049: English Silver Hanukah Lamp,
circa 1940

Value: $1320
Photo courtesy of Swann Galleries, Inc.

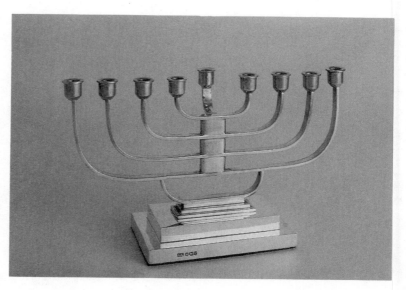

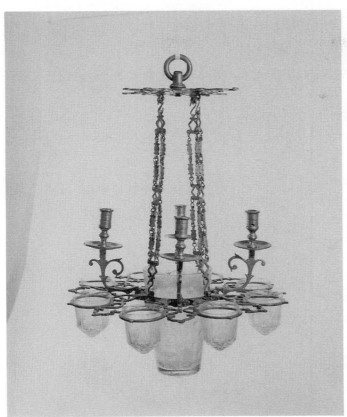

HL050: Rare 18th Century **Indian Brass and Glass Hanukah and Sabbath Lamp**

Value: $7150
Photo courtesy of Swann Galleries, Inc.

HL051: **Stone Maccabee Chanukkiah**, Ellen Lord, hand-cast Durastone, 12" wide

Value: $65
Photo courtesy of Hamakor Judaica Inc.

HL052: **Star Chanukkiah with Music Box**, music box plays Maoz Tsur, solid brass

Value: $55
Photo courtesy of Hamakor Judaica Inc.

HL053: **Ornate Electric Chanukkiah Lions of Judah**, solid brass base, 10-1/2" high

Value: $65
Photo courtesy of Hamakor Judaica Inc.

HL054: A Fine **Silver Hanukah Lamp,** Eastern European, mid-19th Century, central cartouche inscribed in Hebrew with family dedication, indistinctly marked, struck with quality mark 14, 31cm high

Value: $4400
Photo courtesy of Sotheby's Tel Aviv

HL055: A Fine and Rare **Silver Hanukah Lamp, Polish**, early 19th Century, the oil wells with pierced hinged pyramidical covers, struck with quality mark 12, 29 cm high

Value: $14,300
Photo courtesy of Sotheby's Tel Aviv

HL056: A Fine and Rare **Silver Hanukah Lamp,** German, maker's mark MS, Nuremburg, probably 18th Century, centered by Hanukah light blessings, stamped with Nuremburg mark MS within an oval, 21cm high

Value: $15,000 - 20,000
Photo courtesy of Sotheby's Tel Aviv

HL057: A Large and Fine **Silver Hanukah Lamp**, Continental, possible German, 19th Century, 87 cm high

Value: $8000-12,000
Photo courtesy of Sotheby's Tel Aviv

HL058: An Unusual **Bezalel Brass Hanukah Lamp**, 1920's, of semi-circular form, the backplate chased with lions flanking a cartouche inscribed in Hebrew here occured the miracle that lit the candles for eight days', fronted by a conforming base embossed with Hebrew inscription and set with 4 blue stones, fitted with eight removable brass loops holding glass oil receptacles, the whole set on five hemispherical supports, includes matching servant light, 21.5 cm high

Value: $11,000
Photo courtesy of Sotheby's Tel Aviv

Kiddush Cup

KC001: **Venetian Glass Kiddush Cup**, handmade by the famous Artisans of Murano, Italy, blue with 24k gold trim, other side decorated with seven-branched Menorah, 5-1/2" high

Value: $65
Photo courtesy of Hamakor Judaica Inc.

KC002: A **German Silver Gilt Festival Kiddush Cup**, Johann Carl Stiebeldy, 1737-1739, the octagonal cup chased with regence panels of bell flowers within strap work below Hebrew inscription, set on a knopped and conforming circular base with matching ornament, marked on cup and base, 13.7 cm high

Value: $11,000
Photo courtesy of Sotheby's Tel Aviv

KC004: Left - A **Polish Silver Goblet**, early 19th Century, the plain tulip-form cup set on a baluster stem and domed circular base, stamped with quality mark 12, 15.6 cm high.
Value: $693
KC005: Right - A **Polish Silver Kiddush Goblet**, early 19th Century, tulip-form cup engraved with a diamond pattern set on a faceted knop and stepped square base stamped with stars, stamped with quality mark 12, 11.3 cm high
Value: $1000 - 1200
Photo courtesy of Sotheby's Tel Aviv

KC003: A **Dead Sea Stone Kiddush Goblet,** late 19th Century, of tulip form, inscribed and chased with floral decoration, Holy Land vignettes and Hebrew presentation of "Pinhas Katan, Jerusalem", set on a domed circular base, some damages, 14.3 cm high
Value: $3740
Photo courtesy of Sotheby's Tel Aviv

KC006: A **German Silver Kiddush Cup**, maker's mark MH conjoined, circa 1670, the hexagonal cup chased with a band of hearts above a Hebrew inscription for the Sabbath, set on a faceted double knopped stem, the domed circular base with further heart motifs, full marked, 18.5 cm high

Value: $5720
Photo courtesy of Sotheby's Tel Aviv

KC007: A Fine **German Silver Kiddush Cup**, maker's mark PS in an oval, mid-18th Century, the octagonal cup chased with a band of flowers above fluting, engraved with Hebrew Sabbath inscription, set on a faceted baluster stem and domed circular base chased with rocaille, marked on cup and base, 15 cm high

Value: $7000-9000
Photo courtesy of Sotheby's Tel Aviv

KC008: A **German Silver Kiddush Cup**, Nuremberg, probably Joh. Nic. Wollenberg probably 1766-69 or 90-94, of octagonal form, five inscribed with a single line of Hebrew characters and one facet inscribed with three lines of Hebrew characters, the interior guilt, repaired at join of stem and is dome of foot, marked on body and foot, the Hebrew inscription translates as follows: "Remember the Sabbath day to keep it Holy. Sabbath the day for God". 13.1 cm high

Value: $5000-7000
Photo courtesy of Sotheby's Tel Aviv

KC009: An Important **German Silver Gilt Kiddush Cup**, maker's mark HE, Augsburg, 18th Century, inscribed in Hebrew "Pessach, Matzah, Marrah", marked, 21.1 cm high

Value: $20,000-30,000
Photo courtesy of Sotheby's Tel Aviv

KC010: **A German Silver Kiddush Cup,** E. Hechtler, circa1900, the bowl chased with fruit clusters, engraved with Hebrew Sabbath inscription, the stem and domed circular base with further fruit decoration, minor repairs, 12.5 cm high
Value: $2530
Photo courtesy of Sotheby's Tel Aviv

KC011: Personalized **Pewter Kiddush Cup** features a hand-engraved Star-of-David.   5-1/2" high

Value: $45
Photo courtesy of Hamakor Judaica Inc.

KC012: **"Traditions" Kiddush Cup.** Jewish artisans of Yemenite, Russian and Ethiopian heritage have come together in an Israeli workshop to fashion fine ritual art, including this heirloom. Decorated with the Hebrew wine blessing, grapevines and delicate Yemenite trim. Sterling with 24K gold plate. 5" high
Value: $150
Photo courtesy of Hamakor Judaica Inc.

KC013: Silver **Kiddush and Havdalah Goblet** y Ilya Schor, late 1950's

Value: $6000
Photo courtesy of Swann Galleries, Inc

KC014: A **Silver-gilt Kiddush Cup**, Polish, circa 1820, inscribed and dated in Hebrew 1824, indistinctly marked, struck with quality mark 12

Value: $3000-4000
Photo courtesy of Sotheby's Tel Aviv

KC015: A **German Silver Kiddush Cup**, Johan F. Ehe, Nuremberg, late 18th Century, the tulip-form bowl engraved with Hebrew inscription and flowers, chased with half fluting, set on a octagonal knopped stem and circular base with rocaille decoration, marked on foot rim, 14 cm high
Value: $7150
Photo courtesy of Sotheby's Tel Aviv

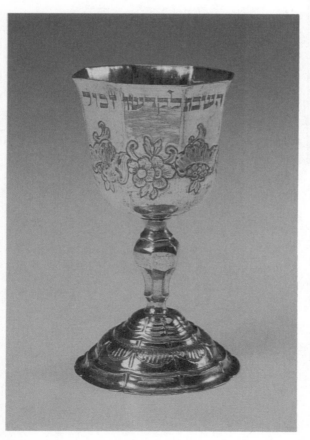

KC016: A **Silver Festival Kiddush Cup**, German, Franz Christoph Mederle, Augsburg, 1761-63, engraved with Hebrew inscription "remember the Sabbath day to keep it holy", the interior gilt, 11 cm high

Value: $11,500
Photo courtesy of Sotheby's Tel Aviv

Pictures

JP001: **The Last Night of the Hanukah Light** by Charles Spencelayh, signed, oil on canvas, 50.6 x 40.6 cm

Value: $24,000
Photo courtesy of Sotheby's Tel Aviv

JP002: **The Promised Land** by Charles Spencelayh, signed, oil on canvas, 49.3 x 39 cm

Value: $27,000
Photo courtesy of Sotheby's Tel Aviv

JP003: Hand-Painted Etching **"City of Peace"** by Amram Ebgi, depicts a dove winging over Jerusalem, filled with Ebgi's characteristic detail, etching is also embellished with intaglio Hebrew calligraphy and copper medallion, pencil-signed edition of 200 on BFK Rives paper, printed in Israel, image 16" x 26" paper 22" x 29-1/2"

Value: $475
Photo courtesy of Hamakor Judaica Inc.

JP004: **In The Bet Hamedrish**, Alois Koloszvary (Hungarian, early 20th Century), signed oil on canvas, 55 x 68 cm
Value: $5000-7000
Photo courtesy of Sotheby's Tel Aviv

JP005: **House of Learning**, Artur Markowicz (Polish 1872-1934), signed and dated Krakow, 1929 pastel on laid paper, 48.5 x 63 cm
Value: $5000-7000
Photo courtesy of Sotheby's Tel Aviv

JP006: **Rabbis,** Mortiz de Groot, signed oil on canvas, 50 x 71 cm
Value: $6000-8000
Photo courtesy of Sotheby's Tel Aviv

JP007: **Portrait of a Rabbi,** Aloysius Priechenfried (Austrian 1867-1953), signed oil on panel, 9.1 x 12.2 cm
Value: $3000-5000
Photo courtesy of Sotheby's Tel Aviv

JP008: **Abraham, Sarah and the Three Angels**, Abel Pann (Russia-Israel 1883-1963), signed twice and inscribed Etude pastel on laid paper, 45.5 x 60.5 cm

Value: $15,000-20,000
Photo courtesy of Sotheby's Tel Aviv

JP009: **Fete de Purim,** Lucien Philippe Moretti, signed oil on paper laid down on canvas, 46 x 38 cm

Value: $3000-4000
Photo courtesy of Sotheby's Tel Aviv

JP010: **Mending the Nets,** Jozef Israels, signed watercolour heightened with gouache and gum arabic, 50 x 80 cm; 19-5/8 x 31-1/2"
Value: $30,000-40,000
Photo courtesy of Sotheby's Tel Aviv

JP011: **The Seamstress,** Jozef Israels, signed oil on panel, 22.8 x 15.9 cm;   9 x 6-1/4"

Value: $8000-10,000
Photo courtesy of Sotheby's Tel Aviv

JP012: **View of the Temple Mount**, Jerusalem, signed and dated 1865, oil on canvas, 32.5 x 43 cm; 12-3/4 x 17"
Value: $14,000-18,000
Photo courtesy of Sotheby's Tel Aviv

JP013: **A Woman Praying**, Oppler (German 1867-1929), signed and dated 1911, oil on canvas, 91.5 x 72 cm

Value: $10,00-15,000
Photo courtesy of Sotheby's Tel Aviv

JP014: **Heimatlose (Homeless)**, Wilhelm Wachtel (Viennese, 1875-1942), signed and dated 1915, oil on canvas, 34.5 x 45 cm

Value: $7150
Photo courtesy of Sotheby's Tel Aviv

164

JP015: A Panoramic View of Jerusalem, Eugen Bracht (German 1842-1942), signed and dated 1915, oil on canvas, 34.5 x 45 cm

Value: $7150
Photo courtesy of Sotheby's Tel Aviv

JP016: **The Thinker**, Zvi Ribak (Russian-Israeli), signed, oil on canvas, 49 x 45 cm

Value: $9900
Photo courtesy of Sothebey's Tel Aviv

JP017: **Portrait of a Rabbi**, Zvi Ribak (Russian-Israeli) signed, oil on canvas, 39 x 34 cm

Value: $8800
Photo courtesy of Sotheby's Tel Aviv

JP018: **Havdalah Zvi Malnovitzer** (Israeli), signed, oil on canvas, 100 x 81 cm

Value: $5500
Photo courtesy of Sotheby's Tel Aviv

JP019: **Portrait of Eleazar Herschel**, Jozef Israels, signed lower left, oil on canvas, back dated 1858 and initialed J.I., 37.5 x 45 cm

Value: $9900
Photo courtesy of Sotheby's Tel Aviv

JP020: **A Jew Near the River** - Taschlich Samuel Hirzenberg (Polish, 1865-1908), signed, oil on board, 34 x 23 cm

Value: $6600
Photo courtesy of Sotheby's Tel Aviv

JP021: **Portrait of a Rabbi**, Otto Eichenger, signed, oil on board, 26 x 19.5 cm

Value: $1980
Photo courtesy of Sotheby's Tel Aviv

JP022: **Portrait of Rabbi**, David Sinzheim (1745-1812), Anonymous, early 19th Century, oil on canvas, original gilt frame, 32.5 x 24 cm

Value: $9250
Photo courtesy of Sotheby's Tel Aviv

JP023: **Portrait of Dr. Rathenau,** Lesser Ury, signed; Nachlass mark on the stretcher and Nachlass oil on canvas, 53 x 71.1 cm; 20-7/8 x 28"

Value: $20,000-30,000
Photo courtesy of Sotheby's Tel Aviv

JP024: **The Street of the Chain**, Jerusalem, C. Cubitt, signed, dated 1887 and inscribed Jerusalem in Hebrew, watercolour, 38 x 30.4 cm; 15 x 12"

Value: $4000-6000
Photo courtesy of Sotheby's Tel Aviv

JP025: **Jerusalem**, T. M. Templeton (English School, 19th Century), signed and dated April '89, oil on canvas, 25.4 x 46 cm; 10 x 18-1/8"

Value: $6000-8000
Photo courtesy of Sotheby's Tel Aviv

JP026: **"Seated Man"** signed and dated '05, oil and gouache on paper laid down on board, 35 x 28 cm

Value: $5000-7000
Photo courtesy of Sotheby's Tel Aviv

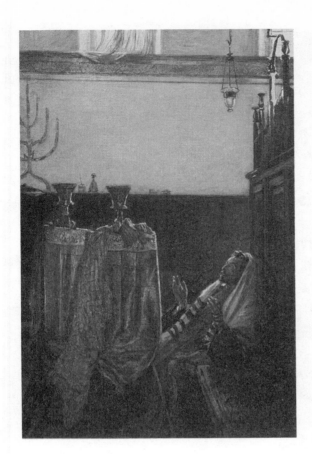

JP027: **"The Prayer"**, Ismael Gentz, signed and dated 1904, oil on canvas, 63 x 43 cm

Value: $7000-9000
Photo courtesy of Sotheby's Tel Aviv

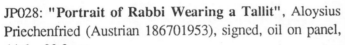

JP028: **"Portrait of Rabbi Wearing a Tallit"**, Aloysius Priechenfried (Austrian 186701953), signed, oil on panel, 44.6 x 33.3 cm
Value: $5000-7000
Photo courtesy of Sotheby's Tel Aviv

JP029: **"Deborah"**, Wilhelm Wachtel, oil on board, 58 x 44.5 cm

Value: $2500-3500
Photo courtesy of Sotheby's Tel Aviv

173

JP030: **View of Jerusalem**, Ludwig Blum, signed and dated 1960, signed in Hebrew, oil on canvas, 73 x 116.2 cm; 28-3/4 x 45-3/4"

Value: $12,000-15,000
Photo courtesy of Sotheby's Tel Aviv

JP031: **Jerusalem Street Scene**, Ludwig Blum, signed and dated, Jerusalem 1961, signed in Hebrew, oil on canvas, 73.5 x 60.2 cm; 28-7/8 x 23-3/4"

Value: $5000-7000
Photo courtesy of Sotheby's Tel Aviv

JP032: On the Balcon, Maurycy Gottlieb (Polish 1856-1879), oil on canvas,
32 x 24 cm

Value: $30,000-40,000
Photo courtesy of Sotheby's Tel Aviv

JP033: **Winter in Litauen,** Jokob Steinhardt (Berlin-Jerusalem 1887-1968) signed with
initials and dated 1919, signed, titled and dated 1919 on the reverse, oil on canvas,
65 x 51.2 cm

Value: $12,000-15,000
Photo courtesy of Sotheby's Tel Aviv

JP034: Portrait of a Yeshiva Student, Isidor Kaufmann, signed oil on panel, 23 x 16.5 cm

Value: $60,000-80,000
Photo courtesy of Sotheby's Tel Aviv

JP035: **Homeless**, Maurice Minkowski, signed oil on canvas, 80 x 200 cm

Value: $20,000-30,000
Photo courtesy of Sotheby's Tel Aviv

JP036: Reading by the Window, Isidor Kaufmann (Austrian 1853-1921), signed, oil on panel,
18 x 13.5 cm.
Value: $60,000-80,000
Photo courtesy of Sotheby's Tel Aviv

JP037: **The Rabbi,** Mane-Katz, signed oil on canvas, 35 x 27 cm; 13-3/4 x 10-5/8"

Value: $18,000-25,000
Photo courtesy of Sotheby's Tel Aviv

JP038: **Moses,** Lesser Ury (Berlin 1861-1931), signed oil on board, 83 x 69 cm

Value: $20,7000
Photo courtesy of Sotheby's Tel Aviv

JP039: **Scene from the Shtetl-recto Biblical Scene-verso,** Jakob Steinhardt (1887-1968), signed with the initials and dated 1920-recto oil on canvas, 95 x 75 cm

Value: $25,000-35,000
Photo courtesy of Sotheby's Tel Aviv

JP040: **Yom Kipper Prayers**, Leopold Pilichowski (Polish-English 1864-1933), signed oil on canvas, laid down on board, 29 x 43.5 cm

Value: $18,000-25,000
Photo courtesy of Sotheby's Tel Aviv

181

JP041: Joseph and His Brothers, Lesser Ury, (Berlin 1861-1931), signed and dated 1919, oil on canvas, 100 x 70.4 cm

Value: $11,500
Photo courtesy of Sotheby's Tel Aviv

JP042: **Rebecca,** Lesser Ury (Berlin, 1861-1931), signed and dated
1908 lower left, oil on canvas, 102 x 69 cm

Value: $40,000-60,000
Photo courtesy of Sotheby's Tel Aviv

JP043: **Man Praying with Lulav and Etrog**, Michel Adlen, **signed;** signed, titled and dated Paris 1962 on the stretcher, oil on **canvas,** 40 x 60 cm

Value: $1500-2000
Photo courtesy of Sothebys Tel Aviv

JP044: **Portrait of Three Rabbis,** Artur Markowicz (Polish, 19th Century), signed upper left and dated Krakow 1923, oil on board, 36 x 51 cm.
Value: $8250
Photo courtesy of Sotheby's Tel Aviv

JP045: Interior of Synagogue in Jerusalem, Harold Copping,
signed, gouache and watercolour, 68.5 x 44 cm

Value: $13,000-16,0000
Photo courtesy of Sotheby's Tel Aviv

Sabbath Items

SB001: A **Polish Silver Beaker**, circa 1841, the sides chased with foliage beneath leaf bands enclosing a deer and lion flanking a cartouche engraved in Hebrew: This is the cup (made) 'shmirot', underside struck with quality mark 12 and dated mark 1841, 6 cm high

Value: $1430
Photo courtesy of Sotheby's Tel Aviv

SB002: A **Polish Silver Sabbath Beaker**, mid 19th Century, the faceted body engraved with a broad band of scrolling foliage above a cartouche engraved in Hebrew 'Shabbat Kodesh', minor damages, the underside stamped with maker's mark and later Hungarian hallmark, 7 cm high

Value: $770
Photo courtesy of Sotheby's Tel Aviv

SB003: A **Viennes Silver Passover Cup**, maker's mark RD, late 19th Century, the body stamped in relief with a continuous frieze depicting the Exodus from Egypt with Hebrew title, the interior Gilt, fully marked
6.1 cm high.

Value: $1980
Photo courtesy of Sotheby's Tel Aviv

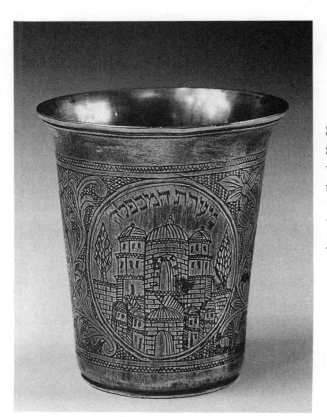

SB004: A **Holy Land Silver Beaker**, Sfat, late 19th Century, Th[e] sides engraved with three Hebrew titled architectural vignett[es] within oval reserves alternating with flowers and foliage, underside stamped with quality mark 12, 6.5 cm high

Value: $2000-3000
Photo courtesy of Sotheby's Tel Aviv

SB005: **Bezalel Silver Passover Dish**, Jerusalem, 1928, designed by Ze'ev Raban

Value: $4180
Photo courtesy of Swann Galleries, Inc.

SB006: Rosewood and Silver Sabbath Plate and Silver and woodhandled **Hallah Knife** by ilya Schor, late 1950s

Value: $13,200
Photo courtesy of Swann Galleries, Inc.

Spice Towers

ST001: A **German Silver Tower-form Spice Container**, marker's mark E.B. in rectangle, Nuremberg, late 18th Century, the square mid-section with pierced rosette windows and hinged door, tooled with another door, windows and corner stones below a platform, pennants at the angles, and cylindrical spire tapering to a filigree finial and simulating tiles, on a circular base flat chased with foliage, later finial, small split to foot rim, 21.2 cm high

Value: $4500
Photo courtesy of Sotheby's Tel Aviv

ST002: A **Hungarian Silver and Filigree Spice Tower**, maker's mark V.M., Budapest, early 19th Century, the square spice section and hinged door with foliate scrolls between twisted columns and pennants at the angles, above a shaped spire terminating in an orb and flag finial, on a knopped stem and domed base, 30 cm high
Value: $8000
Photo courtesy of Sotheby's Tel Aviv

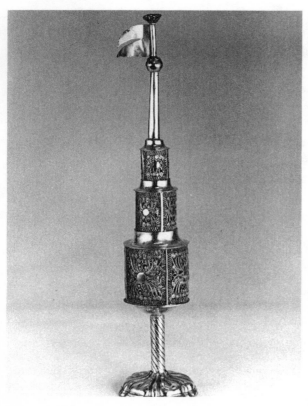

ST003: A **Silver and Filigree Spice Tower**, East Prussian or Polish, early 19th Century, the body composed of three spools in sizes with filigree panels and wrigglework borders, the largest fitted with door, surmounted by a tapering knopped spire and pennant finial, on a spirally fluted stem and shaped circular ribbed and lobed base, unmarked, 29cm high

Value: $1300
Photo courtesy of Sotheby's Tel Aviv

ST004: Left - A Near **Eastern Parcel-gilt Silver Pomegranate form Spice Container**, Turkish or Balkan, early 19th Century, the fruits in sizes with hinged lids, the larger pierced, on a chased oval base and three scroll supports, unmarked, 12.5 cm high
Value: $1200-1500

ST005: Right - A Near **Eastern Parcel-gilt Silver Pomegranate form Spice Container**, Turkish or Balkan, mid 19th Century, composed of two containers in sizes with hinged lids, on foliate stems, shaped bases and three leaf supports, Tughra marks, 11cm high
Value: $1200-1500

Photo courtesy of Sotheby's Tel Aviv

ST006: A **Dutch Silver Stork-form Spice Container,** Rotterdam, 1910, standing with one foot aloft on a circular base applied with frogs, the body hinged, the beak holding a snake, button eyes, 27.5 cm high

Value: $1200-1500
Photo courtesy of Sotheby's Tel Aviv

ST007: Left - A **Silver and Filigree Spice Tower** probably East Prussian or Polish, late 19th Century, the container of hexagonal form with stylized foliate scrolls and wriggle-work borders hinged door, above a tapering knopped spire and pennant finial, on a spool stem and circular base, the pennant later, unmarked, 25.7 cm high
Value: $800

ST008: Right - A **German Silver Spice Tower,** Berlin, circa 1830, the cylindrical body pierced with an interesting pattern between stamped borders, hinged door, surmounted by two similar sections below a spire and finial, on a circular base, marker's mark rubbed, 21.6 cm high
Value: $1700

Photo courtesy of Sotheby's Tel Aviv

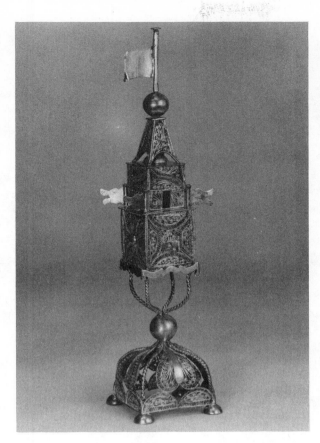

ST009: A **Silver and Filigree Spice Tower** probably Polish, mid-19th Century, with a square spice section and hinged door above a moulded apron, the filigree incorporating wrigglework, pennants at the angles, the tapering spire with a similar finial, on a twisted wire stem and domed base, 27.5 cm high

Value: $1300
Photo courtesy of Sotheby's Tel Aviv

ST010: A **German Silver Spice Tower**, late 18th Century, the square spice section tooled with a chess-board pattern and a clockface above the hinged door, with a detachable spice tray and cover, the top applied with a pierced balustrade and pennants at the angles, tapering knopped spire and flag finial, on a circular pedestal base, stamped L., and standard mark 13, 22cm high
Value: $17,000
Photo courtesy of Sotheby's Tel Aviv

ST011: A **Polish Silver Spice Tower** late 18th Century, the rectangular compartment pierced with lions and strapwork, alternating with stylized flowerheads and scrolls, twisting pillars at the angles below a frieze incorporation lions and a tapering spire tooled to simulate tiles, monster mask finial, on a rectangular platform, knopped stem and circular domed base chased with panels of birds and foliage, unmarked, 22cm high

Value: $4000
Photo courtesy of Sotheby's Tel Aviv

ST012: Left - An **Austro-Hungarian Silver and Filigree Spice Box**, late 19th Century, of square form, with pennants, at the angles below a spire and flag finial, on a wire stem and base conforming in outline, replaced door, 21 cm high
Value: $450

ST013: Center - **Polish Silver Filigree Spice Tower**, early 19th Century, of typical form, surmounted by a spherical knop, on a leaf tipped platform set over a twisted wire stem and square base, lacking door and pennant finial other losses, unmarked, 18 cm high
Value: $600

ST014: Right - A **Polish Silver Spice Tower**, Pogorzelsky, Warsaw, 1890, the concave cubic spice section surmounted by lions below a spire hung with bells and pennant, on skirted stem and square base, later door and pennant, 24.2 cm high
Value: $1,500

Photo courtesy of Sotheby's Tel Aviv

ST015: An Israeli **Gold and Gem-Set Bird and Flower-Form Spice Tower**, Moshe Smilovici, Tel Aviv, 1950's in the form of a bird with movable wing revealing a hollow spice holder, set on a floral bouquet, the flowers set with various stones, set into a wicker-work flower pot above a braided stem and domed square base with leaf decoration, the upper section mounted 'en tremblant', 13.2cm high

Value: $3000
Photo courtesy of Sotheby's Tel Aviv.

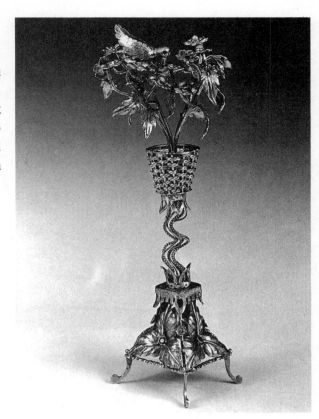

ST016: A **German Silver Havdalah Candleholder and Spice Container**, marker's mark IGH in a trefoil (Rosenberg No. 4291), Nuremberg, circa 1770, the domed scalloped base and stem fitted at mid-point with a square drawer, the interior with four compartments, below a movable candlesocket set on four wires, terminating in a drop guard and suspension ring, the suspension ring slightly later, the stem damaged at the join to the base, mark on base and drawer tap, 21.5 cm high
Value: $8250
Photo courtesy of Sotheby's Tel Aviv

ST017: A **German Silver Spice Tower**, probably Berlin, circa 1870, the square filigree central section fitted with a door, surmounted by pennants, spice and larger pennant, on tapering cylindrical stem and domed circular base with engine turned bands 25.5 cm high

Value: $825
Photo courtesy of Sotheby's Tel Aviv

ST018: An Unusual **German Silver Spice Tower**, late 19th Century, conceived as a central cylindrical flower pierced with stylized scrolling foliage, one side fitted with a door applied with small flowers some surmounted by Stars-of-David (some lacking), set on a fluted knop stem and domed circular base, this example was evidently inspired by the Moorish influence evident in Synagogue architecture in Germany at that time, 23 cm high

Value: $3740
Photo courtesy of Sotheby's Tel Aviv

ST019: A **Silver Filigree Spice Tower**, apparently unmarked, probably Polish, mid-19th Century, the octagonal mid-section hung with bells and surmounted by eagles at the corners, the hexagonal spire set with prancing deer and pennants at the corners, the whole surmounted by a sperical knop and larger pennant, all on a skirted domed circular base and flat octagonal base, 26.5 cm high

Value: $3520
Photo courtesy of Sotheby's Tel Aviv

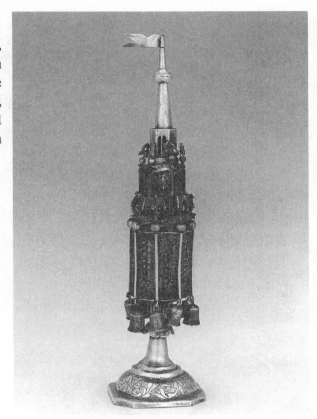

ST020: An Unusual **Continental Silver Spice Tower**, apparently late 19th Century, the cylindrical midsection engraved with foliage and Star-of-David with pierced pull-off lid, surmounted by a pennant, on a knopped stem and scroll-stamped circualar base, 21 cm high
Value: $1900
Photo courtesy of Sotheby's Tel Aviv

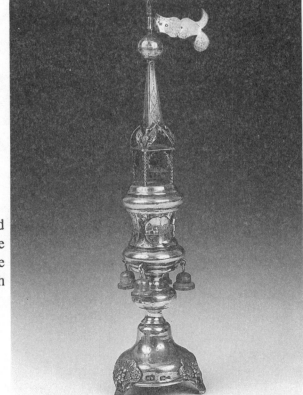

ST021: A **Polish Silver Spice Tower**, Warsaw, 1889, the solid spool-form mid-section fitted with a door surmounted by a spire applied with eagles and hung with a bell, a large pennant above the knopped stem hung with four bells, on a domed circular base with grapevine support, 27 cm high

Value: $1540
Photo courtesy of Sotheby's Tel Aviv

197

ST022: A **German Silver Spice Tower**, maker's mark Korok (?), Berlin, circa 1860, with filigree central section fitted with a door and applied with pennants, surmounted by Prussian eagle and larger pennant over a bell-form frame (bell now lacking), all on fluted knopped stem and matching base, 29 cm high

Value: $1870
Photo courtesy of Sotheby's Tel Aviv

ST023: A **Polish Silver Spice Tower, cum Havdalah Candleholder**, mid 19th Century, the octagonal filigree mid-section set on a knopped domed conforming base with leaf tips, the removable spire and pennant fitted for insertion of Havdalah candle, minor damage, 22 cm high

Value: $1500-2000
Photo courtesy of Sotheby's Tel Aviv

ST024: Right - An Unusual **Continental Silver Filigree Spice Tower**, probably Polish, mid 19th Century, the square spice section with flower heads, one opening as a door, the spire applied with cartouche-form panels, surmounted by pennant, set on a twisted wire stem with spherical knop and square base, apparently unmarked, 17.8 cm high
Value: $1650

ST025: A **Polish Silver Spice Tower**, Kanczucki, Czernowitz, 1863, the square filigree mid-section fitted with a door set in galleried rim surmounted by four pennants surrounding a central bell hung in a spire with larger pennant knop, set on a wire-work stem with spherical knop and square filigree base with hemispherical supports, 23.5 cm high
Value: $1100

Photo courtesy of Sotheby's Tel Aviv

ST026: Left - A Large **Polish Silver Filigree Spice Tower**, mid 19th Century, the square central spice section fitted with a door, surmounted by a spire and small pennant with larger pennant knop, the pennants engraved with German presentation inscription dated 1913, set on four wire-work stems with spherical knop and domed square base on hemispherical supports, bells now lacking, some repairs, 29.5 cm high
Value: $3300

ST027: Right - A **Polish Silver Filigree Spice Tower**, mid 19th Century, composed ot two tapering square sections surmounted by a spire and pennant, the lower section with a door set on four wire-work stems with spherical knop above a square base and hemispherical supports, pennant struck with quality mark 12, the base with Rumania inscription, 26 cm high
Value: $1650

Photo courtesy of Sotheby's Tel Aviv

ST028: Left - An **East European Silver Filigree Spice Tower**, mid 19th Century, of typical low grade alloy, the filigree central section fitted with a door, surmounted by a spire and pennant, hung with bells (two now lacking), on wire-work stem with spherical knop and domed petal-form base (old repairs), 21.5 cm high
Value: $1200-1500

ST029: Right - An **East European Spice Tower**, mid 19th Century, of typical low grade silver alloy, the central filigree spice section fitted with a door, surmounted by a spire and pennant, set on a wire-work stem with circular knop and square base, 22 cm high
Value: $1400-1600

Photo courtesy of Sothbey's Tel Aviv

ST030: A **Polish Silver Spice Tower**, early 19th Century, the square central section pierced and chased with windows and a jug amidst foliage and flowers, one side fitted with a door with peaked roof, the corners with pennants (two now lacking), also lacks top most knop, on baluster stem and domed square base, 16.2cm high

Value: $2750
Photo courtesy of Sotheby's Tel Aviv

ST031: A **Polish Silver Fruit-form Spice Container**, late 18th Century, in the form of a pear with integral stem knop, the lower section pierced and chased with foliage, apparently unmarked, 14 cm long

Value: $2500-3500
Photo courtesy of Sotheby's Tel Aviv

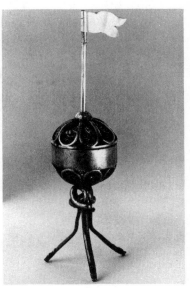

ST032: A **Polish Filigree and Silver Spice Container**, early19th Century, the spherical body with petal-shaped panels and a plain girdle, pennant finial, on three snakes supports, their tails forming the stem, unmarked, 14 cm high
Value: $2100
Photo courtesy of Sotheby's Tel Aviv

ST033: A **Polish Silver Spice Tower**, circa 1830, the square spice section with cut corners, pierced with a flowerhead and foliage, the similarly chased spire surmounted by a later pennant, on a knopped stem and stepped circular base, stamped 12, 15 cm high
Value: $1700
Photo courtesy of Sotheby's Tel Aviv

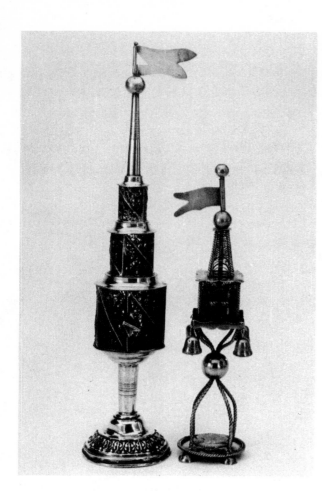

ST034: A **German Filigree and Silver Spice Tower**, Berlin, circa 1845, composed of three openwork spools in sizes, a door fitted to the largest, with a tapering spire, orb and pennant finial, on a similar stem and circular base stamped with leaf tips, maker's mark rubbed, 27.5 cm high
Value: $1000

ST035: A **Continental Silver-gilt and Filigree Spice Tower**, probably Austrian, early 19th Century, the rectangular compartment fitted with a door and hung with bells, rising to a tapering spire and knopped pennant finial, on an orb and wire stem, the circular base with a polychrome enamel of Aaron in the temple, raised on pad supports, 19.5 cm high
Value: $2100

Photo courtesy of Sotheby's Tel Aviv

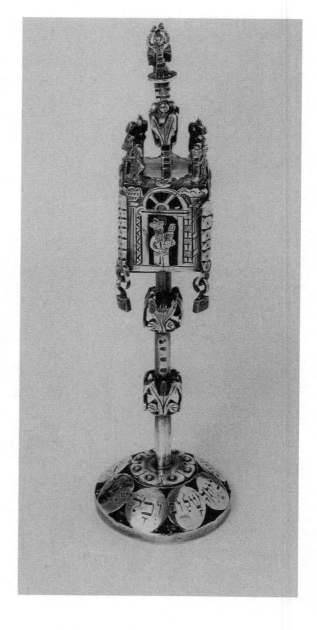

ST036: Silver Spice Tower by Ilya Schor, late 1950's

Value: $17,600
Photo courtesy of Sotheby's Tel Aviv

ST037: **Austro-Hungarian Silver Spice Towers**;
1st tower, late 19th-early 20th Century $412 (left)
2nd tower, 19th Century $880 (right)

Photo courtesy of Sotheby's Tel Aviv

ST038: **A Polish Silver Spice Tower**, circa 1830, the square spice section chased and pierced with leaves and scrolls enclosing a pierced rondel, the sides with twisted columns (pennants lacking), the roof chased in a diamond pattern surmounted by a rampant lion holding aloft a pennant, set on a knopped stem and domed square base, bearing later marks, 20 cm high

Value: $2860
Photo courtesy of Sotheby's Tel Aviv

ST039: A Fine and Large **Parcel-gilt Silver Filigree Spice Tower**, Polish or German, mid 18th Century, later replacement door and lion pennant, bell hung interior, 37.2cm high

Value: $7700
Photo courtesy of Sotheby's Tel Aviv

ST040: A Fine **Parcel-gilt Silver Filigree Spice Tower**, continental, circa 1800, a hinged door at one panel, un-marked, 30 cm high

Value: $15,000-25,000
Photo courtesy of Sotheby's Tel Aviv

ST041: A Fine and Rare **Silver Spice Tower**, Italian, maker's and assay master's marks CL and FB, Venice or Padua, late 17th/early 18th Century, fitted with a hinged door, some repairs, fully marked, 28 cm high

Value: $18,000-22,000
Photo courtesy of Sotheby's Tel Aviv

ST042: A Rare and Important **East European Parcel Gilt Silver and Enamel Spice Tower**, possibly Hungarian, 16th/17th Century, 19 cm high

Value: $48,300
Photo courtesy of Sotheby's Tel Aviv

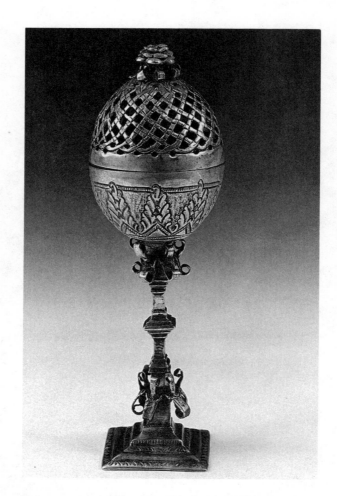

ST043: An Italian Silver Fruit-Form Spice Container, circa 1800, the upper section pierced and chased with scrolling foliage, opening at mid-section, with foliate finial, set on a leaf-applied knopped stem and domed square base, 17cm high

Value: $4620
Photo courtesy of Sotheby's Tel Aviv

Statues

JS001: Leonid Vladimirovitch Posen. **A Russian Bronze Group**, late 19th Century, of a Rabbi on his way to the Zaddik the Sabbath, signed in Latin Sculp., Posen(3)?, Favr. C.F. Woerffel/St. Petersbury, foundry seal rich brown patination, on a faceted brass base, 56 cm wide
Value: $9500
Photo courtesy of Sotheby's Tel Aviv

JS002: **A Group of Five Continental Carved Ivory Figures**, circa 1920, each full figure depicting a Jewish man with a beard and various head gear in full length coat, gesticulating as in conversation, sat on ebonized circular wood plinths, height of figure 9.5 cm., average height overall 14 cm
Value: $3000-4000
Photo courtesy of Sotheby's Tel Aviv

JS003: "Hora Dancers" Statue by Klara Sever, hand cast and hand finished
Durastone on Formica base, 11-3/4" high

Value: $150
Photo courtesy of Hamakor Judaica, Inc.

JS004: "Ten Commandments" by Yigal, beautiful red and blue robe, the brilliant dyes are part of the clay, not painted on the surface, from Israel

Value: $125
Photo courtesy of Hamakor Judaica, Inc.

JS005: "L'Chaim" Statue by Yigal, signed, 13-1/2" high

Value: $125
Photo courtesy of Hamakor Judaica, Inc.

209

JS006: **A German Painted Ceramic Caricature Group**, mid19th Century, depicting four men engaged in conversation, a goat nearby on an integral base painted polychrome with greys and greens predominating, the front with paper label title 'Kinder Israel' and pseudo Hebrew inscription, some damages,
22cm. long
Value: $2640
Photo courtesy of Sotheby's Tel Aviv

JS007: **A Russian Painted Bisque Figure of a Jewish Man**, Gardner factory, late 19th Century, dipicting a man in a long coat, wearing a scull cap and holding an umbrella, standing on a square mossy plinth, painted in black, white, flesh-colour, brown and green, painted factory mark in red, impressed numeral 4,
22.5 cm high
Value: $1760
Photo courtesy of Sotheby's Tel Aviv

JS008: **An Czechoslovakian Painted Ceramic Caricature Group**, circa 1920, depicting two men in conversation, one in traditional Jewish garb, the other in contemporary European dress, the underside with impressed inscription "made in Czechoslovakia" and maker's initials J.M.S., 29 cm high

Value: $1760
Photo courtesy of Sotheby's Tel Aviv

Torah

TX001: **Heavy Silver Filigree Torah Crown**, Warsaw, late 19th Century, the central section composed of straps and flower heads with wriggle work borders, further flower heads and scroll baskets below a smaller crown and cast eagle finial, hung with bells, fitted with stave holders, 44 cm high
Value: $4500
Photo courtesy of Sotheby's Tel Aviv

TX002: A Pair of **German Silver Torah Finials**, circa 1845, the pear-form upper sections applied with foliate and flower-stamped, surmounted by similar crowns and melon finials, hung all round with bells, on simple tapering cylindrical staves, unmarked; and a cream silk Torah Binder, woven in gilt-metal thread with symbols and Hebrew names of the Twelve Tribes, flanking a Decalogue within a foliate scroll reserve, the Torah finials 31.6 cm high, the Torah Binder 60 cm wide
Value: $2700
Photo courtesy of Sotheby's Tel Aviv

TX003: A Pair of **German Parcel-gilt and Silver Torah Finials**, late 19th Century, of baluster form with three, embossed and chased with scrolls and flower heads, two knops pierced and hung with bells, surmounted by eagle finials, on plain staves, 44 cm high

Value: $2900
Photo courtesy of Sotheby's Tel Aviv

TX004: A Pair of **German Parcel-gilt and Silver Torah Finials**, Andreas Mielach, Augsburg, 1805, of stepped circular form, applied with leaf mounts separating pierced galleries and hung with bells, the crown finials surmounted by lions holding inscribed plaques, stiff leafage chased above the cylindrical grips, 31 cm high, case (3)

Value: $11,000
Photo courtesy of Sotheby's Tel Aviv

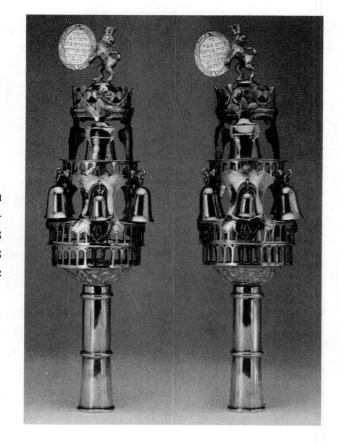

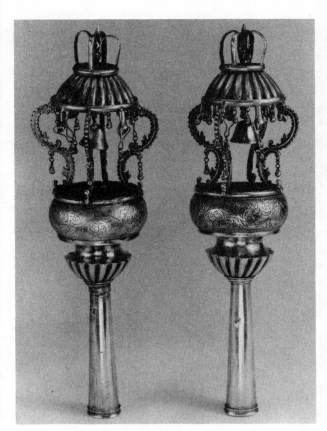

TX005: A pair of **Silver Torah Finials**, probably Salonican, 19th Century, the bulbous bodies chased with foliage above fluted knops and tapering staves, supporting beaded scroll bracket with domes matching the knops and headed by crown finials, unmarked, 33 cm high

Value: $2000
Photo courtesy of Sotheby's Tel Aviv

TX006: An **Italian Silver-mounted Parchment Torah Scroll**, early 19th Century, the scroll finely written, mounted on a silver roller, the handles entwined with snakes, fitted with a later cloth mantle, now in a gilt stamped roan case, 11 cm high, 20 cm overall
Value: $35,000
Photo courtesy of Sotheby's Tel Aviv

TX007: A **Polish Silver-cased Esther Scroll**, circa 1800, the cylindrical case applied with three cast, chased and pierced foliate bands, baluster knops at the ends and on the thumb piece, unmarked, the scroll finely written on parchment,   9 cm high, the case 16.5 cm

Value: $2300

Photo courtesy of Sotheby's Tel Aviv

TX008: A **Pair of Moroccan Silver Torah Finials,** early 20th Century, of pear-form chased and pierced with foliage, hung with bells from bird's heads, surmounted by crowns and set on scale patterned staves, some bells lacking, stainless steel chains, 36 cm high
Value: $1600
Photo courtesy of Sotheby's Tel Aviv

TX009: A Pair of **Dutch Parcel-gilt Silver Torah Finials,** mid-18th Century, the faceted lower divisions pierced and chased with panels of foliage, on plain staves, surmounted by three-tiered six-sided baluster sections, pierced and with rocaille decoration and hung with bells, headed by crowns, the central tiers applied with the Hebrew words KETER TORAH, apparently unmarked, some damage and old repairs, 45.5 cm high
Value: $17,000
Photo courtesy of Sotheby's Tel Aviv

TX010: A **Pair of Unusual Silver Torah Finials**, probably Turkish, mid 19th Century, in Galician style, each composed of a spirally fluted, also with flowers and scrolling foliage, surmounted by an openwork bell-hung crown, chased with leaf tips and flowers, eagle finial, on a domed circular base similarly decorated, unmarked, 38 cm high

Value: $2200
Photo courtesy of Sotheby's Tel Aviv

TX011: A **Pair of Silver Filigree Torah Finials**, Continental, circa 1800, the hexagonal bodies pierced with arches and hung with bells, pierced balustrades at the bases, the tooled grips applied with scroll brackets, surmounted by tiled roofs and double crown finials, two bells detached, 35.5 cm high

Value: $3500
Photo courtesy of Sotheby's Tel Aviv

TX012: A **Continental Silver Passover Plate**, possibly Portuguese, mid 18th Century, of shaped circular form, the central depression engraved in Hebrew with the Passover portions in roundels headed by a crown, at the border the Hebrew word PESACH and foliage, moulded and beaded rim, small rim, small splits, 23.7 cm diameter

Value: $1000-1500
Photo courtesy of Sotheby's Tel Aviv

TX013: **A Heavy Silver Torah Pointer**, probably Austrian, mid-19th Century, the upper half of the tapering stem faceted between orb knops, the lower section in the form of an arm applied with a band of stylized foliage, pointing hand and gathered cuff, chain, unmarked, 31 cm long

Value: $1000
Photo courtesy of Sotheby's Tel Aviv

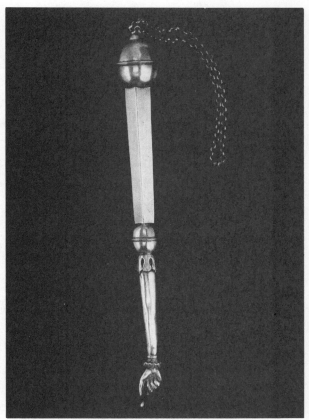

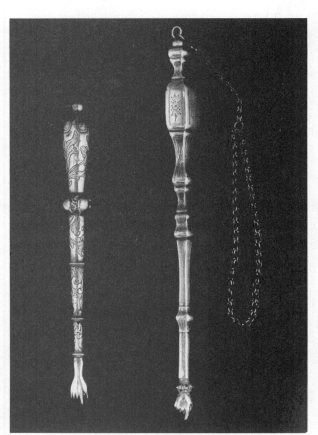

TX014: **An Austro-Hungarian Silver Torah Pointer**, Vienna, 1847, the knopped stem with three corded bands, chased with leaves, and lobes below the ring finial, chain, 25 cm long
Value: $1900

TX015: **An Austro-Hungarian Silver Torah Pointer**, circa 1880, the faceted stem with a baluster section below the knob and ring finial, tooled with flowers and wriggle work at the borders, chain, 32 cm long
Value: $800-1200

Photo courtesy of Sotheby's Tel Aviv

TX016: **A German Parcel-gilt and Silver Torah Shield**, Franz Anton Gutwein, Augsburg, 1798-99, of architectural form with fluted draped pillars and rampant lions flanking a central scale decorated panel overlaid with Hanukkah lamp and alter surrounding the Decalogue and compartment for the festival plaques, at the base a ribbon tied wreath inscribed in Hebrew and dated, hung with three bells, associated, the drape cresting surmounted by an openwork crown, chains, and a festival plaque, 38 cm high
Value: $1000

TX017: **A German Silver Torah Shield**, Frankfurt A.M., circa 1798, of cartouche form, the border embossed with husks and flowers enclosing rampant lions and a coronet above a Hebrew inscription and a compartment for festival plaques, hung with five bells, and a chain with oval hook similarly embossed, marked on shield and hook, markers' mark rubbed; and eight plated Festival Plaques, 23 cm high
Value: $7000

Photo courtesy of Sotheby's Tel Aviv

TX018: An **Unusual Silver Torah Shield,** probably Austrian, circa 1840, embossed and chased with lions flanking the Decalogue below leaves and crown cresting, lion masks and scrolls forming the rim, chain, unmarked, 31.8 cm high
Value: $1200
Photo courtesy of Sotheby's Tel Aviv

TX019: **A Polish Silver Torah Shield,** circa 1820, of rectangular form with oval cresting, embossed and chased with incurved tulip pricked pillars below birds, centered by a basket of flowers above a Decalogue, shell and scroll borders, moulded rims, apparently unmarked, 24.2 cm high
Value: $1200
Photo courtesy of Sotheby's Tel Aviv

TX020: **A German Silver Torah Shield,** circa 1830, the shaped rectangular back plate chased with latticework and applied with pillars surmounted by cast eagles, centered by an applied screen-form Decalogue and lion supporters between a frieze and container for the festival plaques, and rope borders, similar cresting chains and bells, also including four festival plaques, unmarked, 34 cm high
Value: $1000
Photo courtesy of Sotheby's Tel Aviv

TX021: **A Parcel-gilt and Silver Torah Shield,** probably Austrian, last quarter of the 18th Century, of rectangular form, the central section embossed with a vacant rococo cartouche above a compartment for the festival plaques surmounted by lions and deer, flanked by pillars, the crown cresting enclosing the Decalogue, chased foliate borders, chains, unmarked, 21 cm high
Value: $4500
Photo courtesy of Sotheby's Tel Aviv

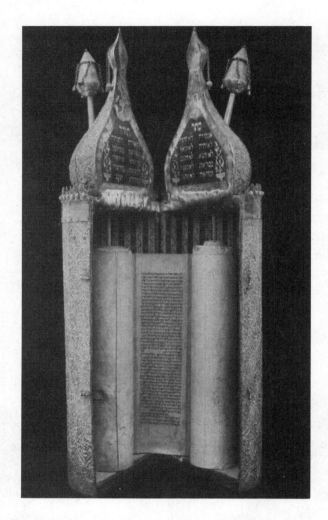

TX022: **An Iraqi Silver Mounted Wood Cased Torah Scroll,** late 19th Century, the case with typical saz leaf-form cartouches embossed with floral clusters, the upper section applied with a later presentation inscription, the interior fitted with Torah scroll below two plaques inlaid in mother-of-pearl with further Hebrew inscription, the top hung with pendants and fitted with a pair of associated near-eastern Torah Finials, 1900, width of scroll 52.5 cm, height overall 110 cm

Value: $1900
Photo courtesy of Sotheby's Tel Aviv

TX023: A Rare Pair of French Parcel-gilt Silver Torah Finials, Paris 1803-09, each with crown-form upper section cast, chased and pierced with strap work, foliage and paired lions, fitted with bells on the outer rim, a larger bell in the interior, surmounted by a circular knob, set on a plain stave holder with foliate and beaded borders, 23 cm high

Value: $26,400
Photo courtesy of Sotheby's Tel Aviv

TX024: **A Pair of Continental Silver Gilt Torah Finials,** probably Polish, late 19th Century, each with crown form upper section fitted with deer heads with holding bells and surmounted by Decalogue, lion and Star-of-David finial, the bulbous lower section fitted with matching deer heads and bells, set on plain cylindrical stave holders with Hebrew inscription, some losses and minor repairs, 45.5 cm high

Value: $2000-2500
Photo courtesy of Sotheby's Tel Aviv

TX025: **A Pair of Bezalel Silver Torah Finials,** early 20th Century, the stave etched with grapevine motifs and Hebrew inscription "Bezalel Jerusalem 1912", surmounted by three filigree spheres hung with two rows of pendants and matching knob, some minor losses and repairs, 33 cm high

Value: $1500-2000
Photo courtesy of Sotheby's Tel Aviv

TX026: **Two Ottoman Silver Torah Finials**, probably Turkish, late 19th Century, each with pear-form upper sections, similarly decorated with panels of flowers and foliage hung with pendants and set on a spherical knob and cylindrical stave holder, 31 cm and 30.5 cm hig

Value: $1540
Photo courtesy of Sotheby's Tel Aviv

TX027: **A Pair of Czech Silver Torah Finials**, Bruenn (Brno) 1810, the columnar stems applied with a band of berried foliage, on a domed circular base with leaf tip border, surmounted by an open crown hung with three bells, one set of bells somewhat later, fully marked, 26 cm hig

Value: $4180
Photo courtesy of Sotheby's Tel Aviv

223

TX028: **A Pair of Austro-Hungarian Silver Torah Finials,**
Troppau, early 19th Century, the cylindrical stems engraved with
alternating bands, surmounted by an open crown with leaf tip base
and spherical knob, all on domed circular base with further leaf tip
border, some damages and losses, 18.5 cm high

Value: $2200
Photo courtesy of Sotheby's Tel Aviv

TX029: **A Polish Parcel-gilt Silver and Filigree Torah Shield,**
mid-18th Century, of square outline with arched top, the surface
applied with filigree and a crown above the Decalogue, with
foliate border, losses, 19 cm high

Value: $4950
Photo courtesy of Sotheby's Tel Aviv

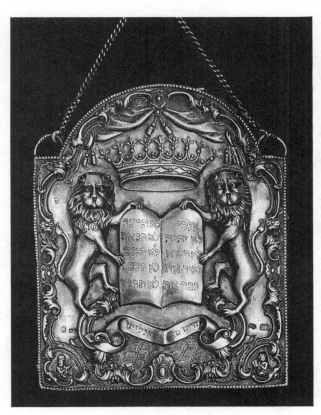

TX030: An Unusual Russian Parcel-gilt Silver Torah Shield, marker's mark D.P. in cyrillic, Moscow 1851, of square outline with domed top embossed and chased with lions flanking the Decalogue beneath a crown above a ribbon engraved with Hebrew name, the borders chased with scroll work forming two cartouches depicting Moses and Aaron, fully marked, 17.3 cm high

Value: $4840
Photo courtesy of Sotheby's Tel Aviv

TX031: A Continental Silver Plated Metal Torah Shield, probably Alsace Lorraine, circa 1900, the foliate chased border enclosing pillars flanking a crown with portion plaque holder fitted with six plaques, engraved with lengthy Hebrew presentation inscription lacks bells and suspension chain, 28.5 cm high

Value: $1320
Photo courtesy of Sotheby's Tel Aviv

TX032: **An East European Parcel-gilt Torah Shield**, Rumanian or Polish mid 19th Century, the arched square embossed and chased in relief with pillars and foliage, applied with lions flanking the Decalogue below a crown above plaque holder and heart-shaped, engraved below further Hebrew inscriptions including the date 1851, lacks suspension chain, apparently unmarked, 30 cm high

Value: $5500
Photo courtesy of Sotheby's Tel Aviv

TX033: **A Pair of Highly Important Parcel-gilt Silver and Filigree Torah Finials**, probably Dutch, late 17th Century-early 18th Century, inscribed in Hebrew "Crown of Torah" and with Latin family crest, struck with later French Empire control marks (in use 1809-19), 40 cm high

Value: $43,700
Photo courtesy of Sotheby's Tel Aviv

TX034: **A Silver Torah Crown**, Polish Posen, 19th Century, inscribed with Hebrew date equivalent to 1885 and the names of two Synagogue Gabbais and two Boreres, struck with quality mark 12, 38.5 cm high

Value: $10,000-12,000
Photo courtesy of Sotheby's Tel Aviv

TX035: **A Rare Parcel-gilt Silver Finial**, Breslau, late 18th Century, marked, 4.3 cm high

Value: $16,000
Photo courtesy of Sotheby's Tel Aviv

TX036: A fine **Silver Torah Crown**, Italian, 19th Century, 9.5 cm high

Value: $7000-9000
Photo courtesy of Sotheby's Tel Aviv

TX037: **A Large Silver Torah Crown**, Continental, 19th Century, includes Sefer Torah fitments, apparently unmarked, 38.5 cm high
Value: $2500-3500
Photo courtesy of Sotheby's Tel Aviv

TX038: A Silver Torah Crown, Austrian, circa 1870, 29 cm high

Value: $2500-3500
Photo courtesy of Sotheby's Tel Aviv

TX039: A Fine Silver Mounted Wooden Torah Case, possibly Baghdad or Burma, 1916, inscribed inside with dedication date in Hebrew, Torah finials (some bells lacking) possibly earlier, apparently unmarked, 86 cm high

Value: $12,100
Photo courtesy of Sotheby's Tel Aviv

TX040; **A Near Eastern Silver Torah Tik Crown**, possibly Libyan, late 19th Century, composed of nine panels, each embossed and chased with foliage enclosing urns of flowers above a Hebrew inscription, hinge pins surmounted by moulded bud-form knops,   82 cm long

Value: $4400
Photo courtesy of Sotheby's Tel Aviv

TX041: **A Silver-gilt Torah Crown**, Italian, 19th Century, embossed and chased with Hebrew quotations, name of Rabbi Chaim ben Aharon Benisho and date equivalent to 1887, apparently unmarked, 20 cm high

Value: $4000-6000
Photo courtesy of Sotheby's Tel Aviv

231

TX042: **An Italian Parcel-gilt Silver Torah Crown**, apparently unmarked, early 19th Century, composed of six foliate arches surmounted by a fruit-form knob, the lower section composed of a band pierced and chased with rococco-style scrolling foliage above a plain band bearing a Hebrew dedication inscription 'for the Torah from the brothers of the Norcci family in the year 1851, 47 cm high

Value: $13,000
Photo courtesy of Sotheby's Tel Aviv

TX043: An Important and Rare Diamond, Ruby and Emerald Set Parcel-gilt Silver Torah Shield, Amsterdam, 1899, inscribed in Hebrew: "This Torah was written by Yaacov Lavarden (of blessed memory) from Holy Community of Rotterdam from the family of great Rabbi Moses Uri (of blessed memory) in his name & memory stood up to a descendent Yosef Isaac son of Jacob Levi Jocobson who funded the donation of the silver tass filled with precious stones in the honor of this Torah on his 60th birthday 10 Iyar (year equivalent to) 1899", 17.7 cm high

Value: $15,000-20,000
Photo courtesy of Sotheby's Tel Aviv

TX044: **A Pair of Silver Gilt Torah Finials,** Berlin, Friedrich Wilhelm Borcke, circa 1820, on bell lacking, fully marked, 29.3 cm high

Value: $5000-7000
Photo courtesy of Sotheby's Tel Aviv

TX045: **A Pair of Unusual Parcel-gilt Silver and Filigree Bimah Fixtures,** Bulgarian, inscribed in Hebrew "This silver for fastening (in) Beit Hakneset Ohev Shalom in the year (equivalent to) 1891", 44.5 cm high

Value: $8000-12,000
Photo courtesy of Sotheby's Tel Aviv

TX046: **A Pair of Parcel-gilt Silver Torah Finials**, Italian, early 19th Century, each set with five cartouches applied with silver-gilt Temple attributes, etched in Hebrew on one inside cover 'Moses Levi in societa coi suoi Fratell', 33 cm high

Value: $15,000-20,000
Photo courtesy to Sotheby's Tel Aviv

TX047: An Important Parcel-gilt Silver Torah Crown (Atarah), Italian, circa 1810-20, applied with gilt reliefs within oval cartouches of the Menorah, the Temple Alter, the Shewbread, the Decalogue and ritual washing utensils, one gilt gemstone-form application lacking, one foliate upper crest lacking and one with old restoration, apparently unmarked, 21 cm high

Value: $25,000-35,000
Photo courtesy of Sotheby's Tel Aviv

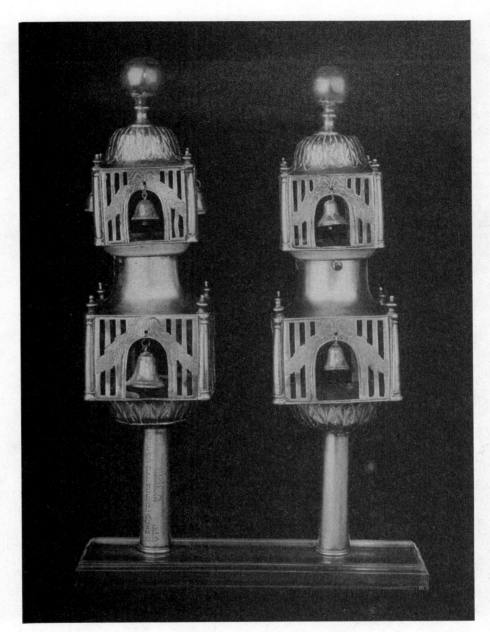

TX048: A Pair of Important Parcel-gilt Silver Torah Finials, Berlin, Casimir Ernst Burcky, early 19th Century, one stave inscribed in Hebrew with presentation inscription and date equivalent to 1808, some bells lacking, marked, 38.6 cm high

Value: $15,000-20,000
Photo courtesy of Sotheby's Tel Aviv

TX049: An Important Pair of Miniature Parcel-gilt Silver Torah Finials, probably Amsterdam, early 18th Century, staves struck with later Dutch tax marks, 18 cm high

Value: $12,000-18,000
Photo courtesy of Sotheby's Tel Aviv

TX050: **A Metal Mounted Wooden Torah Case,** Iraq, 1892, inscribed on outer sections with presentation inscriptions, inner sections richly decorated in watercolor and inscribed with Hebrew date equivalent to 1892 and verse relating to the upraising of the Torah Scroll, includes Torah Finials inscribed in Hebrew with presentation inscriptions, fitted with Torah Scroll,   Torah Finials: 22.5 cm high   Scroll: 51.2 cm width
 95 cm overall

Value: $8,000-12,000
Photo courtesy of Sotheby's Tel Aviv

TX051: **A Fine Parcel-gilt Silver Torah Shield,** maker's mark FD, possibly Franz Dorfmeister, F. Domhart or F. Dominjk, Vienna 1859, with Moses and Aaron flanking the Decalogue, presentation inscription, marked and stamped G. Simon in two places, 38 cm high

Value: $10,000-15,000
Photo courtesy of Sotheby's Tel Aviv

TX052: **A Fine Iraqi Silver-mounted Wood Case Torah Scroll,** mid 19th Century, of typical cylindrical form, the tik covered in silver, chased with rosettes within quatrefoil reserves, each side decorated with two crowned Decalogues flanking a menorah composed of Hebrew psalms over a representation of the Temple, Hebrew inscriptions at the borders, surmounted by a baluster knob hung with fish pendants, staves for finials, now lacking, the interior fitted with a Torah Scroll below silver plaques with Hebrew inscriptions, Scroll: 46 cm Case: 91 cm high

Value: $12,000-15,000
Photo courtesy of Sotheby's Tel Aviv

240

TX053: A Rare Polish Silver Torah Shield, apparently unmarked, mid 18th Century, the rectangular shield embossed and chased with lions beneath a crown flanking a canopy, the sides decorated with rococco-style scrolling foliage and flowers, fitted at intervals with colorful pastes, the center painted with a bride and groom beneath glass (cracked), above a Hebrew inscription flanking two zodiac signs in Hebrew titles of Taurus and Capricorn, the base hung with three bells, the top with suspension chain and winged cherub knob 18 cm high

Value: $5500
Photo courtesy of Sotheby's Tel Aviv

TX054: An Unusual Polish Silver Torah Shield, first quarter 19th Century, of shaped circular outline, the border chased with flowers, scroll work and a crown, enclosing lions flanking a heart-shaped shield above a small rectangular shield, both engraved with Hebrew inscriptions, one dated 1814 recording its presentation in the town of Mihaliczer (?), 21 cm high

Value: $4400
Photo courtesy of Sotheby's Tel Aviv

TX055: **A Polish Silver Torah Shield**, probably Warsaw, circa 1840, of cartouche form embossed and chased with lions flanking the Dacalogue within pillars amidest scrolling foliage, below an eagle and crown, the center with revolving dial engraved with Hebrew names of holidays, struck with marker's mark JOSIPH and quality mark 12,   23.5 cm high

Value: $3300
Photo courtesy of Sotheby's Tel Aviv

TX056: **A Polish Torah Shield**, second half 18th Century, of very low grade silver, square with arched top, the beaded border enclosing scrolling flowers and foliage surrounding a central rectangular plaque, decorated above with unicorns centering a roundel engraved with Hebrew initials for crown of Torah, 18.5 cm high

Value: $1760
Photo courtesy of Sotheby's Tel Aviv

TX057: **A German Parcel-gilt Torah Shield**, G. Hetzler, Berlin, late 18th Century, of cartouche outline, the borders chased with rococco scrolls enclosing pillars and urns with lions crowning the Decalogue above the portion plaque holder applied on a trellis and diaper ornamented ground, suspended with three bells below, 27.5 cm high

Value: $6380
Photo courtesy of Sotheby's Tel Aviv

TX058: **A Continental Parcel-gilt Silver Torah Shield**, probably Rumanian or Polish, mid 19th Century, embossed and chased with pillars flanking lions surmounted by a crown and an eagle, enclosing the Decalogue and portion plaque amidst scrolling foliage enclosing a ram above a line of Hebrew inscription, some minor losses, apparently unmarked, 27 cm high

Value: $5060
Photo courtesy of Sotheby's Tel Aviv

TX059: **A German Parcel-gilt Silver Torah Shield**, possibly Berlin, circa 1870, the square shield embossed and chased with scrolling foliate border enclosing pillars flanking applied lions, crown Decalogue and portion plaque, all on a trefoil ground, the bottom hung with bells, 30 cm high

Value: $1760
Photo courtesy of Sotheby's Tel Aviv

TX060: **A Polish Silver Torah Shield**, apparently unmarked, mid 19th Century, of cartouche form embossed and chased with pillars flanking a Decalogue amidst rococo-style scroll work applied with a crown and lions, decorated below with empty portion plaque opening and Hebrew inscription in cartouche dated 1843, 31.5 cm high

Value: $6380
Photo courtesy of Sotheby's Tel Aviv

Auction Houses/Experts

Expert-Judaica
Authur Feldman
1815 St. Johns Ave.
Highland Park, IL 60035
Phone: 312-432-2075

Expert-Judaica
Heller Antiques, LTD.
Israel Heller
5454 Wisconsin Ave.
Chevy Chase, MD 20815
Phone: 301-654-0218
Specializes in jewelry, Judaica silver.

Christie's Auction House
502 Park Ave.
New York, NY 10022
Phone: 212-546-1000

Hamacore Gallery
Chicago, IL
Phone: 708-677-4150

Rita-Mobley Auction Inc.
P.O. Box 531
South Glastonbury, CT 06073
Phone: 203-633-3076
Specializing in Historical items, ephemera (paper prints), autographs, photographs, etc.

Sotheby's
219 E. 67th. St.
New York, NY 10021
Phone: 212-606-7000

Sotheby's Israel Limited
38 Gordon Street
Tel Aviv 63414
Phone: 011-972-(3)-5223822/52469897

Swann Galleries
104 E. 25th. St.
New York, NY 10010
Phone: 212-254-4710
Oldest/Largest U. S. Auctioneer specializing in rare books, autographs, manuscripts, Judaica, photographs, and works of art on paper.

Dealers

Dealer: Judaica
Gary Niederkorn Silver
Newspaper: <u>Silver Edition</u>
2005 Locust St.
Philadelphia, PA 19103
Phone: 215-567-2606
Specializes in 19th & 20th century silver novelties, jewelry, napkin rings, Judaica, picture frames, etc.

Dealer: Judaica
Holy Land Treasures
Suite D
1200 Edgehill Drive
Burlingame, CA 94010
Wants to buy Jewish rare books, manuscripts, documents, antique ritual silver, Hanukah lamps, candlesticks, art, paintings, etc.

Christian: The Autom
5226 South 31st Place
Phoeniz, AZ 85040
Phone: 800-521-2914

Dealer: Judaica
Weschler's
William P. Weschler Jr.
909 E. Street NW
Washington, DC 20004
Phone: 202-628-1281
They have specialized auction sales of art, paintings, prints and graphics.

Christian: Golden Era Sales Inc.
3182 Twin Pine Rd.
Grayling, MI 49738
Phone: 517-348-2610
Buying and Selling Antiques, hats, pre 1960 clothing, rustic and fine furniture, silver, jewelry, estate liquidations, appraisals, house sales conducted on your premises.

Museums/Libraries

B'nai B'rith Klutznick Museum
1640 Rhode Island Ave. NW
Washington, DC 20036
Phone: 202-857-6538

Center for Jewish Art
The Journal: Jewish Art
P.O. Box 4264
Jerusalem 91042, Israel

Judaic Museum
6125 Montrose Rd.
Rockville, MD 20852
Phone: 301-881-0100

Juddah L. Magnes Memorial Museum
2911 Russell Street
Berkely, CA 94705
Phone: 415-849-2710

Morton B. Weiss Museum of Judaica
100 Hyde Park Blvd.
Chicago, IL 60615
Phone: 602-924-1234

National Museum of American Jewish History
55 N. 5th Street
Philadelphia, PA 19106
Phone: 215-923-3811

Plotkin Judaica Museum of Greater Phoenix
3310 No. 10th Avenue
Phoeniz, AZ 85013
Phone: 602-264-4428

Spertus Museum of Judaica
618 S. Michigan Avenue
Chicago, IL 60605
Phone: 312-922-9012

Yeshiva University Museum
2520 Amsterdam Avenue
New York, NY 10033
Phone: 212-960-5390